Herman Charles Merivale

The White Pilgrim, and Other Poems

Herman Charles Merivale

The White Pilgrim, and Other Poems

ISBN/EAN: 9783337292126

Printed in Europe, USA, Canada, Australia, Japan

Cover: Foto ©Thomas Meinert / pixelio.de

More available books at **www.hansebooks.com**

THE
WHITE PILGRIM

AND OTHER POEMS.

BY

HERMAN CHARLES MERIVALE,

AUTHOR OF "FAUCIT OF BALLIOL," ETC.

CHAPMAN AND HALL, Limited,
11, HENRIETTA STREET, COVENT GARDEN.
1883.

TO MY DEAR WIFE,

E. M.

NOVEMBER, 1882.

PREFACE.

I DO not remember in what part of Moore's works I once read the first tremulous remarks he made when, for the first time, he committed a volume of poetry to the world, and appealed to it as a poet. Plays which have only appeared in dramatic form, stray verses which magazines have absorbed, look very different to the writer when first he contemplates them in the ambitious form of a book, and trembles for his own venture. May this find lenient judges and kindly friends. And let me express the hope that the political verses which form part of it may be taken in the spirit in which they are written, of freedom from offence. I have carefully revised them with that view, conscious that expressions which may pass for the moment should have no longer life than *ce que vivent les plaisanteries.*

The title and the MS. prose legend which give their name to this book (first suggested to him, of course, by the oath in "Sintram," though having nothing else in common with it) I owe to the graceful fancy of my friend, Mr. Gilbert à Beckett (in stage phrase my collaborator), when "The White Pilgrim" was acted. Its stage life was not a long one, and under modern conditions could hardly be so. As the writing and the poem are throughout mine, Mr. à Beckett has kindly and readily acceded to my wish to publish it with my other work. I think that I owe it to him in return to say that the willingness with which he trusted a favourite fancy to my care deserved a better return than a stage spoiling.

From any literary view, things on the stage have certainly changed. Authors might put their best literary qualities, in all their differing degrees, into a *School for Scandal, She Stoops to Conquer, Money,* or *London Assurance*—which can always be revived, for old favourites are sacred in England. But nowadays they had better keep them out of plays, and use them elsewhere.

There will always be room for one man, with the intellect and tact of Irving, to keep alive the immortal Shakesperean legend by adapting it to the peculiarities of the day, but— I fear that the rest is silence. Lord Ellenborough is reported once to have said, as a warning to barristers, "There are callings, in which to be suspected of literature is dangerous." I am afraid that the calling of the dramatist is one of them.

November, 1882.

CONTENTS.

THE WHITE PILGRIM.

	PAGE
ACT I.	3
ACT II.	25
ACT III.	45
ACT IV.	62

OCCASIONAL POEMS.

HORACE'S GHOST	83
OLD AND NEW ROME	85
THE WISHES OF A DUMB-WAITER	92
LADY FAIR	95
LA VIOLETTA	97
LONDON LOVES	98
THESPIAN THEMES	101
ÆTATE XIX.	104
EN PASSANT	107
WAKE, ENGLAND, WAKE!	109
THE TWENTY-FOURTH OF MAY	112
A HOME-SIDE STORY	115
MDLLE. CROIZETTE IN "THE SPHINX"	119
"LE SPHINX"	122
"NAY, I'LL STAY WITH THE LAD"	123
A SPRIG OF HEATHER	126
IN TWO WORLDS	130
LES ENFANS DE BOHÊME	133
PEACE—AND HONOUR	136

CONTENTS.

SONGS AND BALLADS.

	PAGE
A LIFE'S REGRET	143
SPINNING-WHEEL SONG	145
"RUBY WINE AND ROSY LIP"	146
MY SECRET	148
SERENADE	149
HORATIAN ODE	150
VENETIAN BOAT-SONG	152
MARIAN MAY	155
ST. VALENTINE'S TOUR	158
READY, AY, READY	162
SIR PAUL'S DAUGHTER	164
BRIAN BORU	165

PARODIES, ETC.

THE TOWN OF NICE	169
MATILDA	171
ANGOT-MANIE	173
THE CRUISE OF THE SIX HUNDRED	175
AD AQUÆ POTORES	178

RHYMES FOR THE TIMES.

A WINTER'S TALE	181
HÄCKEL OF JENA	184
WH—STL—R v. R—SK—N	187
RORKE'S DRIFT	190
"POSTE RESTANTE"	193
THE ROYAL WEDDING	196
BEN-BASTES FURIOSO	202
THE HEART OF MIDLOTHIAN	205
VÆ VICTIS	208
THE STORM	212
BOOK C, ODE I.	217

CONTENTS.

TRANSLATIONS.

	PAGE
REMEMBRANCE	223
THE FIFTH OF MAY	227
SONG OF THE NIGHT	232
FORTUNIO'S SONG	238
THE LEGEND OF THE SWORD-HILT	239

SACRED VERSE.

PALINGENESIS	245
STANZAS	249
A CHRISTMAS MESSAGE	251

THE WHITE PILGRIM.

A Dramatic Poem,

IN FOUR ACTS.

Characters.

HAROLD.

SIGURD
LEOFRIC } (his Companions).
FRIOTH

ROLF (his Foster-brother).

SIR HUGO.

THE LADY ISABELLE.

THORDISA.

GERDA (her Attendant).

THE WHITE PILGRIM.

THE WHITE PILGRIM.

ACT I.

SCENE.—*Exterior of* HAROLD'S *Castle in Finland. The windows of the Banquet-hall of the Castle and a flight of steps leading into the interior are to the left of the scene; to the right, an old Gothic arch, leading to a Chapel beyond. Along the back of the scene runs a turreted walk, overlooking the sea below, which, with a mountainous coast, forms the background. In its centre a rough cairn of stone. Evening.*

(*As the Curtain rises,* GERDA *is discovered watching by the Gothic arch. A psalm is heard from the Chapel.*)

I.

Lord of the life that is born of the grave,
Merciful Spirit, hear us and save !
Shield us from evil, guard us from wrong,
Through the dull sleep of life bear us along;
Wake us at last with the fair and the brave :
Merciful Spirit, hear us and save !

THE WHITE PILGRIM.

II. SONG FROM THE BANQUET HALL.

Ha, ha, ha! the rich wine flashes
    Ruby red:
There's no heat in dead men's ashes;
    They are dead.
Just awhile, for love and laughter,
    Lasts the light;
Seize the day! what follows after,
    Is—the night!

III. PSALM.

Show us the right way, oh, teach us the true!
Merciful Spirit, make us anew!
Raise us to follow, guide us to tread,
Where to the one goal Thy footsteps have led;
Help us the ill we have done to undo;
Merciful Spirit, make us anew!

IV. SONG.

Ha, ha, ha! the grass grows keenly
    From the tomb;
And the night winds whistle keenly
    Through the gloom.
Deep our draught, our slumber deep is;
    Let us fill
To the dead, whose sober sleep is
    Deeper still!

Enter ROLF *from the Castle, looking back.*

ROLF. Ay, drink away; there were more space for brains,
Were there less room for liquor, in some heads.
(*Seeing* GERDA.) But soft! what vision breaks upon
my path?
Gerda, my pretty Gerda!

GER. Not so fast!
Gerda I am, and pretty, but not yours.

ROLF. I took you for an angel.

GER. So I am;
Or so you used to say.

ROLF. Yes, so I did,
And so I do, and so I always will,
Till better knowledge kill the simile.

GER. Then shall that better knowledge never be.
I'll moult no feather of my angel-wing
For such a faithless worshipper as you.

ROLF. Faithless!

GER. Ay, faithless! faithless as your lord
To my dear mistress; faithless as all men
Are to all women. Oh, we know you, sir,
And all the doings of your wicked crew;
That villainous old Sigurd and the rest;
Sigurd the hunchback—Sigurd, the arch-fiend,
In the disguise of some malicious ape!
Sigurd, who makes of Harold what he pleases!
The savage foe of the pure faith that dawns
In morning splendour o'er our darkened land.

ROLF. Not so; when Sigurd would have driven out

        The band of Christian zealots that do hold
        Their meetings in the ruined chapel there,
        He swore he would not have them meddled with,
        Or driven from their eyrie on the rock
        For half his lordship.

GER.   That's a sign of grace
        Beyond my lady's hopes.   Tell her of that;
        She is among them now.

ROLF.   Thordisa there!

GER. Ay; with the morning she and I set forth
        Upon a certain distant pilgrimage;
        And first she prays for him; sweet, innocent soul,
        To waste such breath in vain.

ROLF.   Why does she go?
        And let her half-fledged warrior walk alone
        When most he needs her?   He is but a boy,
        And he wants counsel.

GER.   Why, what can she do?
        He scorns her counsel; with high words of anger
        They parted yesterday; oh, I am shamed
        To think of what he said.

ROLF.   He was but mad
        With a brief madness; for he loves her well;
        As well as I love you.

GER.   I'll believe that,
        If ever the day come when he shall give
        Proof of his love by driving from his castle
        The ribald band that do deface the sun
        With heathen rites and wild debauchery.

Rolf. And will you love me when that day shall come?
Ger. Ay, that I will, and long days afterwards,
And till I die, or you, or both of us;
By every pretty and becoming oath,
I'll love you—just as well as I do now;
Not a bit better!
Rolf.   Mock me as you will,
I yet will draw you to my lure some day;
Or else may the White Pilgrim call for me.
Ger. What's that?
Rolf.   A legend in my family.
Ger. You have a family, and make love to me?
Rolf. My master's family is to me as mine;
I spoke in metaphor.
Ger.   Let that alone:
Plain speaking suits you better.
Rolf.   'Tis a tale
Of terror, Gerda! children tremble still
At the Earl Olaf's vow. 'Twill make you creep.
Ger. I like to creep. Tell it.
Rolf.   Men say that once,
Between this land and distant Normandy,
There raged a bitter feud, which with the years
Was dying slowly out. One of the worst
And the most daring of Lord Harold's race,
Who ruled in these old halls, was feasting high
With kindred spirits; and half mad with wine,
And all the devil in his blood let loose,
He swore in fearful words a fearful oath;

Swore that to Norman hand and Norman life
Men owned nor knightly faith nor fealty;
And that, should foot of Norman knight that day
Cross but the threshold of his castle home,
And seek a knightly hospitality,
Within one month that trusting guest should die,
By his host's hand struck to the earth and slain!
Earl Olaf swore the oath in fearful words,
And, as the mighty rafters rang again
In hollow sound of ominous laughter back,
He called on Death to register the vow!

GER. How very awful!

ROLF.   Is it not? Sit close,
And listen how the legend runs. 'Tis said
That as the last irrevocable words
Fell from his impious lips, a sudden light
Flashed from the chapel window, and there passed
A sad and white-robed figure from its door
In pilgrim guise, but veiled from foot to head,
That with a gracious majesty of gait,
But footfall dumb and printless, glided down,
Halted awhile beside yon cairn of stone,
Then like a clouded shadow passed away
There, where you look!

GER.   How you do frighten me
I cannot listen to such tales as these
Upon the very spot, and yet I feel
I wouldn't lose the rest for all the world!
Come this way, and go on.

ROLF.   Yes, step aside!
    Here comes my master. Leave him here awhile,
    And let him meet Thordisa; we will watch.
    Then like a clouded shadow passed away——
GER. Go on, dear Rolf, go on.

    [*Exeunt. As they go out*, HAROLD *enters from
        the Castle.*
HAR.   What forms were those?
    Methought I saw a woman's figure pass,
    And heard the rustle of a woman's dress.
    Again the fumes of wine—again the dream
    Of the one face whose starry maidenhood
    Shone luminous through my spirit's trackless gloom,
    Until my own mad hand put out the light.

            [*Shouts and laughter within.*

    Ay, riot on, fit mates for such as I!
    I know no fellowship with better things,
    But live as the beasts live, to die like them.
    A God, Thordisa said. Where is He, then?
    There is a Spirit of Evil, that I know,
    For all day long he wantons in my veins,
    Turns every nobler impulse into ill,
    And sins—and sins—and sins. 'Tis he, not I!
    Why, he was stronger than Thordisa's love,
    To which the world without him were as naught:
    He is a thing more living than myself;
    But if there is a God, where tarries He?
    Oh, answer me, thou great dumb oracle,

Pent in the steel-blue vault above my head,
In the vast silence of a world-wide grave!
Is there no key that shall let in the light
On all the imprisoned terrors that surround
The central mystery of life and death?
If thou hast ever answered, answer me!
Answer, I say!

    [*At the last words,* THORDISA *has entered from the Chapel.*

THO.   Harold!

HAR.   What voice was that?

THO. Harold!

HAR.   Is this mine answer? Art thou sent
Out of the misty spirit-world of air
To tell me—that God is? I dare not look
Upon thy face. Thordisa! Can it be
The ghost of a dead love that smiles on me,
Or does the devil of wine fever mine eyes,
And give my love-dream shape to mock at me?
Thou seem'st to tell me I am pardoned.

THO.   How
Hast thou deserved that pardon?

HAR.   'Tis her voice!
Sweet voice, speak on for ever! Though thou come
To call me hence into an unknown world,
I am prepared to go, if 'tis with thee.

THO. Do not mistake me longer; I am one
As mortal and as erring as thyself.

   I am that same Thordisa whom you loved,
   Or said you did—so often—and so well!
   How could I choose but trust you, when you wooed
   With such a magic eloquence of tongue?
   Yet 'twas thy tongue, and not thy heart that spake.
HAR. It was my heart that spake, and not my tongue!
   My tongue is rude, and has not learnt the trade
   Of ready lovers; but my heart made words
   So true, so strong, so tender, for thy sake,
   They burst the barrier of common speech,
   And poured my very soul out at thy foot,
   To trample, spurn, and play with, what you pleased!
   If that thou art Thordisa, leave me not!
   If that thou art Thordisa, stay with me!
   If that thou art Thordisa, be to me
   My genius of good, my draught of health,
   To kill the subtle poison in my blood,
   Which makes me seem so all unworthy thee!
   There is a devil within me, if thou wilt,
   But all I have of good is only thine!
THO. Oh, Harold, rise! you fright me, wayward boy!
   You are as rough—and sunny—as the sea!
   As crystal seeming, yet as changeable!
   How can I trust you? trust is all in all;
   It is the keystone of that arch of love
   Which in its rainbow beauty spans the world!
   Such trust was mine; what did you do with it?
HAR. I know; I know; yet know not how to plead
   That you were ever cold——

THO.   Cold, cold! for shame!
Why, while the red-hot ardour of your love
Was quenched even in the wine which bore it up,
I with my prayers for thee was wearying Heaven,
Which seemed one mirror to reflect thy face!
But pardon me—I speak unmaidenly:
Cold! well, I may have been; but watch the sun
Behind yon bleak heights wake the tremulous dawn,
Ere yet has paled the evening after-glow;—
We northern maidens are not passionate;
Yet is our love like to our summer, Harold—
It may lack colour, but it knows no night.

HAR. Then let the shadow that has blurred our loves
Be but the twilight link 'twixt night and day,
Which softens, not obscures, their radiance.
Oh, thou sweet saint, thou pretty moralist,
Teach me to woo thee as thou wouldst be wooed,
Even in thy loved faith's chosen formulas!

THO. 'Tis the true faith.

HAR.   I know not; it is thine.

THO. Wilt thou then learn it?

HAR.   Ay. Thou knowest not
How often I have communed with the stars
To give me answer; but they seem to me
Like rivets set in the far wall of heaven
To shut all entrance out.

THO.   Oh no! they are
Heaven's portals, Harold, golden gates that stand
Unbarred above to let our prayers in;
Heaven is so near.

HAR.   It seems not so to me.
Perchance I see it through a haze of wine,
Which lends it distance.   Let me learn of thee!
I'll hold no longer with my father's gods,
If they must part us two.   Ask what thou wilt,
So thou wilt be but mine.   Take me, and take
My lands, my wealth, my heritage, my youth,
All that I have and all that I may win;
But let me wear thee as an amulet
Against the powers of evil!

THO.   It may be
That I too hastily left thee.   But, my love,
For that I hold my soul dearer than thee,
That are to me more dear than all the world,
Strive for my sake, strive for one little year,
To be the Harold of thy lady's dream,
Her very true and very upright servant,
Her Christian knight in very word and deed,
To cast the pagan bonds from off thy soul,
Live worthy of thyself—of Heaven—of me—
And, if what simple service I can render
Should in thine eyes seem good, my hand shall follow
The heart that I had almost lost from sight,
So long ago it travelled forth—to thee.

HAR. But for that year, you will not leave me?
THO.   No.
I do not think I could; but for a while
We must be parted; for I go to-morrow
Upon a pilgrimage to a certain shrine,
To which I have been sent——

Har.   Sent?
Tho.   Yes; a sign
Was given me to obey. I shall be back
Before the month is over.

Har.   It will seem
All the long year, till then. I take thy promise;
And, in what words thou wilt, I give thee mine.

Tho. (*taking a cross from her neck*).
Here, take this cross; I give it you to wear
As proxy for that amulet you spoke of,
In token it is only yours. Read there.

Har. (*reading from the cross*).
"Through Life to Death—through Death to Life."
Ay, so.
Thordisa mine, I will be true to thee
Through Life to Death, through Death to Life!

Tho.   Amen!

[*They embrace, and go up the scene.*

Re-enter Rolf *and* Gerda.

Ger. 'Tis a strange legend. Is it really true?
Rolf. I always tell the truth.
Ger.   Here is my lady
In close talk with your master.
Rolf.   Very close.
See, Gerda, what a thing is confidence!
When will you learn such confidence in me?
Ger. When you become as handsome as your lord.
—My lady, it grows late.

HAR.   Peace, envious girl!
Wouldst thou part lovers newly reconciled,
On such an earthly plea?

GER.   My lord, you owe
Much to my pleading, if you knew the truth.

THO.   Yes, Harold, she has ever stood your friend
And mine—dear Gerda!

HAR.   Let me thank her then,
And leave my sign upon her little hand.
                         [*Kissing* GERDA's *hand.*

GER. (*to* ROLF). When will you kiss with such a grace as that?

ROLF. Now, if you'll let me!

THO.   Have you quarrelled too?

HAR.   Nay, pretty Gerda, be not hard with him,
'Tis a right honest fellow, take my word;
And he has better merited of you
Than I of my Thordisa.

GER.   Possibly.
He might be better looking, for all that.

ROLF. Such better looks are for our betters. Rest
Contented with my virtues.

THO.   Gerda, come,
I know you like him well.

GER.   Faith, well enough!
But not so well but that I'll follow you
Where'er you go, dear lady, to the end.

HAR.   Then when she places this white hand in mine,
As she has sworn to me but now she will,
When my year's test is over, follow her
And profit by example.

Tho.   Now, good-bye!
      Thus lovers trifle with the passing hour,
        And find "Good-bye!" so hard a word to say.

Har. Good-bye, beloved, good-bye! for one brief month,
      That I will wear away in thoughts of you;
      None else could lend it wings. Why do I draw
      So ill a presage from so short a parting?
      I should be glad, yet am I sick at heart.

Tho. 'Tis but thy fancy, Harold; be but true
      To me and to thyself, thro' Death, to Life!

                [*Exeunt* Thordisa *and* Gerda.

Har. Farewell, my better angel! as she goes
      I seem to feel the spirit of ill fall on me,
      To darken all her sunlight into gloom,
      And with its mocking echo drown her voice!

          Enter Sigurd *from the Castle.*

Sig. Come, Harold, come! you were not wont to be
      A laggard in your cups. There's Leofric
      Snoring at table, Siegfried underneath it;
      Some fighting, and some kissing, but all do
      Their duty to the wine-cup manfully,
      Except their lazy host. Why, your wine blushes
      A deeper purple than its mother grape
      At such a want of proper courtesy.
      Come in and drink.

Har.   I'll drink no more to-night.

Sig. You'll drink no more? Harold will drink no more!
      Hear that, ye spirits of his forefathers!

Such words must cure, if anything can cure,
Your everlasting deafness. Oh, my boy,
Think of your gallant father's charge to me,
To guard you and to keep you as myself;
To train and perfect you in manly arts!
And so I have. Harold, you know I have!
You wrestle, fight, play, swear—as none else can;
And now you turn your back upon your drink,
The noblest and the manliest art of all!

ROLF (*aside*). At least it has one merit. Drink alone
  Has power to bring the tears to Sigurd's eyes.

HAR. Truce to this fooling, Sigurd. I have said
  I'll have no more of it to-night.

SIG. (*turning on* ROLF).   You knave!
  You wretched, puny, scurvy, sober knave!
  This is your doing; curse your canting ways!
  Because your own infernal little head
  Declines to carry its due weight of wine,
  Others must thirst to please you.

HAR. (*angrily*).   Let him be!
  And listen, Sigurd. I have had to-night
  A glimpse of the heaven you would shut me from;
  The heaven of a pure woman's holy love.

SIG. A woman!

HAR.   Ay; unless Thordisa bear
  Some other name, to show she stands alone
  Above the race of women. I know well
  That in all love for me you think to draw me
  Away from her——

Sig.   A recreant! false to all
        Her country's story and her country's gods!
        A priest of that rebellious heresy,
        That would discrown our royal deities,
        Make women of our men, monks of our heroes,
        And shame of our dear honours! Even here,
        In the great shadow of our fathers' halls,
        Fell Superstition, like a baleful star,
        Misleads and baffles us! A wicked witch!
        A pale-faced heretic!
Har.   Do not blaspheme!
        For I will live a Christian, for her sake.
Rolf.   And so will I for Gerda's.
Sig.   Hold your peace!
        A Christian, you! a fickle, feeble boy,
        Led by the halter of a woman's hair,
        Charmed with the sorcery of a woman's tongue,
        Drunk in the bad wine of a woman's eyes,
        Which cannot touch the palate, and but racks
        The head i' the morning? So, she has been here,
        Your white Thordisa! Wenches are the worst
        Of all men's damning vices—yet she comes
        And preaches you out of good honest liquor,
        And a good honest friend and guardian.
        I hate all women! but by my father's bones,
        Were she a warm frail piece of flesh and blood,
        With a good spice of the devil, I'd forgive you.
Rolf (*aside*). If that's his taste, I must take care of Gerda.
Sig.   But this cold hypocrite——

HAR.   Silence! One more word,
And I forget my father's love for you,
And all the ties between us—I forget
All but the saint at whom your slanderous tongue
Rails all in vain. Your insults pass her over,
As idle darts the warrior armed in proof!
For she is armoured against ribaldry,
Even in the silver mail of maidenhood.
Not for her sake I bid you pause, but mine;
Mine—and your own. Breathe but another word,
And dearly as I love you, we cross swords.

SIG.   Thou most ungrateful and irreverent boy!

                       [*Turning to the Castle.*

What ho, there! Leofric! Frioth! Ludwig! each
And any of you that can stand upright,
Come here, and listen.

Enter LEOFRIC *and* FRIOTH *and* COMPANIONS.

LEO.   What's the matter now?
Is there a fight on hand?

FRI.   I'll bear my part,
And his besides that has no stomach for it.

LEO.   Here's Harold with his sword out!

FRI.   Quarrelsome,
And very drunk, no doubt.

SIG.   And if he were
I would forgive him. Look at him, my comrades!
Look at our pride—our master-spirit—our hero;
Since he last left us, but an hour ago,
He has turned Christian.

Leo.   Christian! What a freak!
Fri.   He really must be very drunk indeed.
        Fear nothing, Sigurd. Put the boy to bed;
        To-morrow morning he'll recant his errors.
Leo.   Or quite forget he'd errors to recant.
Fri.   Come in, my Harold, come, and have some wine!
Har.   When you are sober, I will talk with you.
Fri.   Then may you never talk with me again.
Har.   Sigurd, you know me!
Sig. (*aside*).   Better than you think,
        For a hot-headed and unstable child,
        Who shall forget Thordisa in a trice.
Har.   I would not quarrel with you, and to-night
        We are too heated to be reasonable.
        To-morrow we will speak of this again:
        And now I sheathe my steel; sheathe thou thy tongue.
        (*Aside*). Sweet saint, for thee I rule myself to-night,
        And thus begins my service.
Sig.   Holy sir!
        I am at your orders at what time you will.
Fri.   Is there no fight, then? This is most unfair;
        Who'll have a turn with me?
Sig.   Our Harold's valour
        Is not well primed to-night. He has not drunk
        Enough to make it boil. But he talks big,
        And that is something.
Fri.   Very sad indeed!

LEO.	I've often heard of Christian meeknesses,
	But never thought to meet with them in him.
	Hail, gentle creature!
FRI.	Hail, thou man of peace!
LEO.	Should but the Norman foe come back again,
	He'd find an easy market for his sword,
	When our best warriors turn saints.
SIG.	Not so
	Lord Harold's fathers talked――
HAR.	Unmannerly!
	I dare do anything my fathers dared.
SIG.	I'll lay you a round wager that you dare not—
	A thousand crowns!
HAR.	I take your wager!
FRI.	Bravo!
	Next to a fight I love a bet.

[SIGURD *whispers to* LEOFRIC, *who goes into the Castle, and returns with a large sword.*

ROLF (*to* HAROLD).	My lord,
	Think of Thordisa.
HAR.	So I do. Would she
	Have me insulted thus?
SIG.	I wager then
	That the Lord Harold dares not take the oath
	His bold forefather swore upon the sword
	The oath they call Earl Olaf's.
ROLF.	Oh, not that!
	Why do you call that devilish memory up,
	Tempter?

Sig. *(threatening him).* What means the rascal?
Rolf.   I care not!
    Do what you please; ay, kill me if you will;
    But let not my dear master soil his lips
    With blasphemies like that. He shall not do it
    While I stand by.
Fri.   Then you shall not stand by,
    For I'll proceed at once to knock you down!
Har. Back, Frioth! This is folly. Norman foot
    Has never trod our coast for years.
Sig.   And yet
    You are afraid to take that oath! Pay down
    Your crowns, and write yourself a coward, boy.
Har. Coward! you lie!   *[Drawing.*
Sig.   Oh, you will fight, perhaps,
    But dare not take the oath!
Har.   I dare, and will.
All. Bravo! The oath! The oath!
Rolf.   My lord! My lord!
Har. Silence, I say! I'll not be baited thus.
    Shall I be frighted with a bugbear, made
    To scare a baby with?
Sig. *(giving him the sword).* Here is the weapon!
    I say you dare not do it!
Har.   Listen, then.
Rolf. Oh, Heaven, be deaf to him, and pardon us!
Har. *(lays his hand upon the sword and recites the oath, while the others, except* Rolf, *gather round).*
        By the might of Odin's hand,
        By the light of Odin's brand,

By the trumpet-blast sent forth
On the echoes of the north,
By the thunderbolt of war
Welded by the hand of Thor,
By this falchion's jewelled hilt,
By the blood its blade hath spilt,
Northern valour, Norman guilt,
By its dye of scarlet red,
By the living, by the dead—
Ere the world's unmeasured bound
Once the sun hath travelled round,
Should but foot of Norman fall
In the shadow of my wall,
Yonder moon of silver stain
Shall not wane and wax again,
Ere with sure and secret blow
I will lay that Norman low!
By mine own hand he shall die,
Meed of Norman perjury!
If he fall not so, then Death
Call for me that break my faith!
Hear mine oath, and mark it well;
Be my witness, Death—and Hell!

[*All stand silent in a circle round the sword.* ROLF, *on his knees, gazes back at the chapel. A light appears in the window, and the* WHITE PILGRIM *enters from the chapel, and walks silently down to the stone in the centre at the back, and there pauses, unseen by all but* ROLF. *A bell strikes one.*

ROLF (*aside*). 'Tis the White Pilgrim, and they see him not!
 [*The sound of a horn is heard outside; all start.*
HAR. What sound is that?—a stranger—at the gate?—
And at this hour! Great Heaven!
SIG. What can it mean?
HAR. (*to* ROLF). Go, see who asks admittance.

 [ROLF *goes out. As he goes, the* WHITE PILGRIM *goes off slowly behind the Castle on the opposite side. The others stand grouped, in silence, in the centre till* ROLF *returns.*

Well, what news?
ROLF. A stranger knight—and lady—at the gate!
HAR. Bid them come in.

 [ROLF *introduces* HUGO *and* ISABELLE, *who come forward;* HAROLD *and the others standing back, as in fear.*

HUGO. This is cold welcome, sirs,
For a spent traveller, who has wandered far.
HAR. From what—land—do you come?
HUGO. From Normandy.

THE CURTAIN FALLS.

Between the First and Second Acts a month, all but a day, is supposed to elapse.

ACT II.

SCENE.—*The same. Morning.*

Enter from the Castle SIGURD *and* ROLF.

ROLF. I say it must not be.
SIG.   I say it shall.
      You're a nice knave to preach flat perjury
      To the "good master," whom you whine about.
      I do not like the business, and am sorry
      I ever put him on it; but to waste
      Time in regrets is idle. He has sworn,
      And trifles with his purpose all too long.
      To-morrow ends the month, and the sun sets
      On Harold perjured, or on Hugo dead.
ROLF. And were that all, there were no room for doubt;
      I had rather see him perjured ten times o'er,
      Than turn a murderer for conscience' sake.
SIG. You irreligious dog! An oath is sacred:
      What is a Norman more or less, to that?
      He swore to strike the blow, and strike himself.

>   Would I might do the deed, and that my hand
>   Might save young Harold from the penalty
>   Which must await him if he break the vow.
> ROLF (*aside*). Ay, the White Pilgrim! did I dream that
>   night?
>   Was that pale phantom my embodied fear?
>   No! it was real; I saw it! You speak truly;
>   And, tempter that you are, Lord Harold's life
>   Hangs on the base fulfilment of his vow.
>   Oh, my dear master, must I see thee die,
>   Or live a thing of shame, a traitor, false
>   To hospitable trust, to knightly honour,
>   Outcast from heaven and from Thordisa's love?
> SIG.   That love is out of date.
>   [*Pointing off the stage.*
>
>   Look where he goes
>   With his new charmer—with his dainty sample
>   Of luscious fruit grafted from southern vines
>   Upon our polar ice.   What pretty things
>   He whispers in the little ear, which blushes
>   In proof it listens not! "Sweet Isabelle,"
>   "I never loved till now!" Ay, ay, go on.
> ROLF. You do him grievous wrong; he would not be
>   So light and fickle a thing.
> SIG.   Fickle, not he!
>   Once let a man swear vassalage to women,
>   And he remains so very true to them,
>   That, if the first should leave him for awhile,
>   He must e'en find a second, then and there.

I like this wanton well; for she will arm
Young Harold's hand against her husband's life,
Which stands between their passion and the sun.
The iron is red hot, the furnace full!
And of the flowers that spring from Hugo's grave,
Harold shall weave new chains for Isabelle.
I must go call the Norman to the chase,
His last! Sing on, my love-birds! ere to-morrow
To harsher chords we'll fit your melody.

[*Exit into Castle.*

ROLF. Can such a liar speak truth, and has my lord
So soon forgot Thordisa? No, not he;
I'll not believe it! Courtesy, not love,
Draws him to Isabelle; that man's foul thoughts
Soil purity itself. Her gentle face
Must palsy Harold's arm ere it can strike
At his guest and her husband. Horrible!
Since that accursëd night I live in fear
Lest every moment bring a deed so black
That it would overcast the smiling Heaven,
And from its own dark womb draw lightning down
To scorch us into nothingness! And yet,
What if the vow be broken—if that life
That I, poor slave, have loved and tended so,
Must perish as the forfeit? Many a time
Would I have warned these Normans of their
    danger,
But that I feared their safety were his death.

    Where is Thordisa? Why, thou guardian saint,
    Leav'st thou thy shrine untenanted, when most
    Our knees should wear the stones out at thy foot
    In agony of prayer? I have not dared
    To breathe the fearful secret in the ear
    Of living soul, till she return.

Enter HAROLD *and* ISABELLE *from the shore.* ROLF *watches behind.*

ISA.   Your friends
  Will miss you, my Lord Harold.
HAR.   Gentle lady,
  They have your husband with them as my pledge.
  May I not stay with you?
ROLF (*aside*).   Too close, too close!
ISA. You ask the favour of me rather late.
  Have you not stayed some time?
HAR.   I do not think it.
  In your sweet presence time goes much too fast.
ISA. (*aside*). And other things go quite as fast as time.
  I thought you told me that you never learned
  To flatter, my kind host?
HAR.   I never have.
ISA. Faith, then, it comes by instinct, or by ear.
  There's ne'er a gallant in our Norman court
  Pays compliments so smooth.
HAR.   Am I not rough?
  I always thought so; but would gladly change
  The image of myself my thoughts reflect,
  If they distort it.

Isa.   Good Sir Pagan, no,
I can't deny the roughness; but it makes
The better setting for smooth compliments.
Contrast is always pleasing.

Har.   Then I think
That I should please you well.

Isa.   Perhaps you do;
But change the subject.

Rolf (*aside*).   It is time to change it!

Isa. You said that time flies fast, and you said true;
One month to-morrow since we stormed your
    hold
And took possession. Why do you start so?

Har. (*aside*).
A month to-morrow! Oh, how I have striven
To drown the memory; to think of it
As of an evil nightmare born of wine!
That oath, I dare not break, and cannot keep!
How have I lived since then!

Isa.   What mutter you?
Some Pagan charm against the evil eye?
Am I so dangerous?

Har.   All is dangerous here!
Most dangerous to yourself—to your lord—to me!
There's danger in the sea and in the air,
Danger within the castle, and without,
Danger by day, by night, above, around,
Danger in the eye that drinks your beauty in,
And danger—in the hand that presses yours!

ISA. (*shrinking as he takes her hand*),
  You hurt me! What means this?
ROLF (*coming up to her and speaking rapidly*).
         It means he is right!
  Danger there is—it comes!

  Enter SIGURD, HUGO, LEOFRIC, FRIOTH, &c.

HUGO.   My good Lord Sigurd,
  You do yourself much wrong—our monarchs give
  No truer hospitality than you.
  Good morrow, my brave host. You were stirring early:
  You join the chase with us?
HAR.   No; not to-day.
HUGO. Why is your face so clouded? Isabelle,
  Is there a quarrel between him and you?
ISA. Something has crossed him, sir; I know not what.
  (*Aside to* HUGO) I pray you, Hugo, make him go with
  And I will wait within for your return. [you,
HAR. Fair Isabelle, I am not so much a churl
  As to leave you untended and alone.
  These gentlemen will pardon me, if to-day
  I bear you company.
ISA.   That will not I, then!
  And, good mine host, you have so maimed my hand,
  That I am better tended—by myself;
  While air and exercise will cool your brain,
  Which, I think, needs it. Rolf, come in with me.

    [*Exeunt* ISABELLE *and* ROLF *into Castle.*

THE WHITE PILGRIM.

HUGO. You have your quittance. Come, 'twere sin to tarry;
   See how the hunt of heaven is afoot!
   The clouds that chase each other through the skies
   Vie with the hounds' impatience, and set us
   A great example. 'Tis a day for sport
   To make a hunter of a hermit.
SIG. (*apart to* HAR.)   Harold,
   What mean these looks, man?
HAR.   Do not speak to me!
   You know their meaning.—Friends, I am not well,
   And you must pardon me.
LEO.   Impossible!
   There are some sins past pardon. Shun the chase!
FRI. You ill deserve the bottle if you do.
   My life upon it that he means to stay,
   And have a morning drink all to himself.
   Harold, this is not fair, upon my soul.
HUGO. Let me entreat you, friend.
SIG.   Leave him to me;
   I know his moods, Sir Knight, and will persuade him,
   Ere you have passed the mountain, to put by
   This gloomy humour.
LEO.   Come, then, to the chase.
       [*Exeunt all but* HAROLD *and* SIGURD.
SIG. Harold——
HAR.   Begone and leave me, tempter! fiend!
   Do I not know you? I can read your face,
   And speak the words in which your lips would hiss
   Their poison in mine ear. The hour is come

When I have sworn to do a thing more vile
Than e'er the vilest did, and write myself
More vile than they, than villany, than thou!
But—I have sworn it! Sigurd, you have been
My guardian, father, and, I thought, my friend.
Is there no way but this? I am ill-taught,
Uncultured, rude of spirit and of speech,
But I have loved you—you, and one beside!
Thordisa, my good angel, come to me!
I dare not think of her, or I go mad!

SIG. Think not of her, then. I am sorry, boy,
To see you thus—I am sorry that my tongue
Outran my sense that night, and laid this oath
Upon your soul—but, Harold, it is there!
I never thought of it save as a jest.

HAR. Then as a jest let me but pass it by.

SIG. It may not be—you know it! After all,
The Heaven you grope your way so blindly after
Must have a purpose on this Norman's life,
Or it had never sent him here so pat.
And what is a man's life, that you should make
So much ado about it? Every day
Your Heaven takes many lives, with much less
    cause,
And just as blindly, here and there, by chance!

HAR. Blasphemer!

SIG.   Nonsense; it's philosophy.

HAR. But this man is my guest; his hand and mine
Have clasped each other; and the wife he loves——

Sig. *You* love. More reason; now, it is a sin;
   Then, you may do it freely.
Har.   It is false!
   I do not love her. From my darkened soul
   Thordisa stands severed as by a veil!
   With the good part of me I worship her,
   And that you have robbed me of. My evil self
   Woos this warm beauty's fiery loveliness
   As it woos the wine-cup, for oblivion!
Sig. Then woo her to some purpose, man alive!
   Why, the rich blood that wantons in her cheeks
   Flutters an answering signal to Desire,
   Whene'er you speak with her. She's a glorious prize
   For the bold cruiser in forbidden seas!
   Take heart of grace, man; do what must be done—
   You have delayed too long.
Har.   My guest and friend!
Sig. Who made him so? Had you but kept your vow
   A month ago—not feasted him, and fawned,
   Where you were sworn to strike—he had not been
   Aught but a doomed and alien enemy.
   It must be done to-day!
Har.   There is one day more;
   Let him live till to-morrow.
Sig.   No, to-day.
Har. Well, be it so. I dare not break that oath;
   Its fearful burden's damning monotone
   Appals my sense—I dare not break that oath!
   Oh, were it but to die instead of him,

I would die fifty thousand deaths a day;
But to die perjured is to die accursed,
And to be pointed at in worlds unknown
As he that did the worst the worst can do!
Look down on me, ye spirits of my sires,
See what your faith, your creed, have done for me!
I know no other creed, no better faith!
Thordisa's God is deaf—Thordisa gone.
And I am helpless. I will do this thing!
And as all mercy fails me, I will fill
The measure to the full. I will win that woman,
And riot in her arms, until we two,
Locked in an earthy and abhorred embrace,
Go down together to the lowest deep,
Embosomed in the everlasting fire!
But—you and I are of one blood no more!
And mark me, when we meet beyond the earth,
In whatsoever place lost spirits are,
I will nor touch your hand, nor know your face,
For ever and for ever! In an hour
I will meet you in the wood, at the mountain's foot,
And damn us both at once. Go to our friends,
Bid Hugo look for me in an hour, in the wood!

[*Exeunt severally.* ROLF *has re-entered at the back with* ISABELLE *just at the last words.*

ROLF. An hour! In the wood! You heard the words?
ISA.   I did,
But know not what they mean. Why do you hint

So darkly, man? Speak out, and speak your mind,
If you have got one.

ROLF.   I can scarcely tell
Whether I have or no—whether I am
Or am not—whether anything has been
Or ever will be. What I ought to do
Is quite beyond me, a poor willing knave,
That only seeks to live at peace with men
And women—Gerda most especially.
Oh, where is Gerda, to advise with me?
She ever says there's wisdom in my head,
And thinks that she can find it. I can not!

ISA. I vow, the changes of the northern moon
Give colour to the proverb, that the brain
Turns with its turnings. Both your lord and you
Are strangely out of tune. When first we came,
You greeted us with such scant courtesy
And such odd looks, that we had almost gone,
Wrecked as we were upon your coast, to find
Some other shelter. As the moon grew less
Our cheer grew better. Now she broadens over
The face of Heaven once more——

ROLF.   Ay, ay, that's it.

ISA. *What* is it, in God's name?

ROLF.   Not in God's name,
But in the devil's! More I dare not say
Than I have told you. Keep my master by you,
Encourage him, let him make love to you,
Make love to him—do anything on earth

Save let him join the hunt, or go to-night
To that dark wood he spoke of—dark indeed
With all the shadows of the nether gloom.
(*Aside*). He shall not do the deed; though the white robe
Of that dread visitant enshroud us all,
And make one mighty pall on Nature's face,
In folds to shrivel her!—Look, my lord comes!
I dare not meet him now. Remember well
The charge I gave you—for your husband's life! [*Exit*.

ISA. My husband's life! What can this warning mean?
His wild words strike the key of mine own dread.
All things are savage here; at night, the air
Seems living with strange whispers, which the day
Swells to a louder tone; I seemed to hear
One when he spoke. What would they do with us?
Ah, my young host, beware a woman's wit!
Forewarned, forearmed, they say, and I will throw
About your eyes a mist of witchery,
To which your warlocks, and your imps, and all
Your battery of pagan devilries,
Shall be a common conjuror's clumsy play.
You shall not leave my side to-night, Lord Harold,
Before I know your secrets as mine own.
I am a practised warrior, and in arms.
Here comes the enemy!

Enter HAROLD.

Still muttering charms?

HAR. Charms for the charmer! Ah! I thought the sun
　　　Shone brighter than it did a while ago.
　　　It has come back again to shine on you.
ISA. 　I think the sun is hidden in a cloud.
HAR. Then 'tis because she sees a rival here,
　　　And dares not show her face.
ISA. 　　　　　　　　　　　The sun's a man!
HAR. A woman, on my life! a very woman!
　　　A woman in her light, her warmth, her splendour,
　　　Whose satellites pale before her where she goes.
　　　A woman! for 'tis summer where she lingers,
　　　And winter when she hastens to be gone!
　　　A woman! for she warms one land to life,
　　　Then leaves it for another—blighted—blank—
　　　You are my sun. I love you!
ISA. (*terrified*). 　　　　　　　　Ah!
HAR. 　　　　　　　　　　　　　I see
　　　You are afraid of me—yes, you are fair,
　　　And, I think, pure and good; (*aside*) and what have I
　　　To do with goodness and with purity?
　　　My hand can strike him; soil her it shall not.
　　　Forgive me. I spoke wildly. Fare you well!
ISA. (*aside*). The wood! He must not leave me! Do not
　　　　　go!
HAR. (*aside*). Sigurd was right, then. We are all alike;
　　　Women and men—save one!—I will stay with you
　　　For ever, if you will.
ISA. 　　　　　　　　　That's a long day.
HAR. Is it? I fear it is.

Isa.   You say you love me?
It is a courtly phrase, and means, I know,
No more than fashion. Let us walk this way.
(*Aside*). Will the time never pass?—Why do you start?
Har. It was a sudden gust that stirred the trees.
(*Aside*). Methought Thordisa's voice was on the wind
Wailing a sad good-bye!—You are beautiful!

[*Exeunt behind the Castle.*

Enter Thordisa.

Tho. How slowly heavenward rolls the stream of time
For parted lovers; but how swift the tide,
Slipping in noiseless current out of sight,
When on his full broad breast he bears along
Two happy lives in sweet companionship.
Thus Love points out the quickest road to Heaven,
And Heaven's best angel upon earth is Love.
How will you meet me, Harold? Oh, my soul
Shrinks from its own excess of happiness.
Thou art too much the burden of my prayers,
Too much my incarnate Heaven—too much? Oh, no.
I'll not believe it; 'tis an idle fear
Engendered of the Evil One, who tempts us
To put aside the choicest cup that God
Has offered to our lips. I cannot think
Too much of him that only thinks of me.
To-day, then, I shall see him once again,
And feel once more his kisses on my lips,
And speak with him once more, and once more hear

      The words of the troth-plight he plighted me,
      The words——

ISA. (*without*). Through Life to Death, through Death to
      Life !
THO. A woman's voice ! A woman's !—oh ! no, no !
      My ears deceive me—that way came the sound ;
      I heard it.   [*Looks off the Scene.*
          Ah ! Yes : I did love too much !

             [*She falls back and listens.*

      Enter HAROLD *and* ISABELLE.

ISA. A pretty posy, and a pretty token :
      Who gave it you ?
HAR.   What matter ? It was given me
      By a vision, in a dream, a dream that passed
      So long ago.
THO. (*aside*). One month !
HAR.   Don't speak of it.
      Speak only of ourselves ; there are to us
      No others in the world ; its mighty orbit
      Has not an inch of breathing space save that
      My passion needs. Will you not answer me
      Save with excuses ? Dalliance is well ;
      But there are better things than dalliance.
ISA. (*aside*). I know not what to do ; I am at the end
      Of all my fence.—Nay, but I have a fancy
      That in this text you pledge yourself to me.
HAR. I will not.

Isa. No? Then you have sworn most falsely,
And I will never trust so false a love.
Har. Ask anything but that.
Isa. No other boon
I care to ask. 'Tis but a little thing,
And it means nothing.
Tho. (*aside*). Nothing!
Har. No; not much.
I will buy you at that price—(*Aside*) nor you alone!
—Fair Isabelle, I will be true to thee
Through Life to Death, through Death to Life!

[*Music heard from the Chapel.*

Isa. What's that?

CHANT IN THE CHAPEL.

Pray for the passing soul,
Soft let the death-bell toll
Over the dying;
In the light breeze whose breath
Perfumes the road to death,
Angels are sighing!

Har. I'll have those Christians silenced. I have said it;
And if we need a witness, Death, attend
And take me at my word!
Tho. (*aside*). Ay, come, come, Death!
In the most fearful of the shapes you wear,
Take them and me! Ay, come, thou thing accursed!
Come, terrible phantom! severer of hearts
That beat for thee to blight when hope is highest!

Thou stealthy reaper of the golden grain!
Thou image of the darkness whereupon
Thou sitt'st enthroned! Thou nightmare of the night!
Come with the cruellest weapons that thou hast,
Red-heated from thine awful armoury!
Bring all thy choicest tortures for these two,
And spare me not. Come, fiend!

[*The* WHITE PILGRIM *appears, seen only by* THORDISA; *she throws herself between it and the others.*

                                  Oh, no, not yet!

ISA. It is very cold. Oh, take me from this place;
There is a rush of darkness in the air.
I am afraid.

HAR.   Fear nothing; come with me.

           [*Exeunt* HAROLD *and* ISABELLE.

THO. Spirit, I know thee not. I look on thee
With awe, but not with terror. All my fears
Fall from me as a garment. Art thou—

PILGRIM.   Hush,
Miscall me not! Men have miscalled me much;
Have given harsh names and harsher thoughts to me,
Reviled and evilly entreated me,
Built me strange temples as an unknown God,
Then called me idol, devil, unclean thing,
And to rude insult bowed my godhead down.
Miscall me not! for men have marred my form,

And in the earth-born grossness of their thought
Have coldly modelled me of their own clay,
Then fear to look on that themselves have made.
Miscall me not! ye know not what I am,
But ye shall see me face to face, and know.

  I take all sorrows from the sorrowful,
And teach the joyful what it is to joy.
I gather in my land-locked harbour's clasp
The shattered vessels of a vexèd world,
And even the tiniest ripple upon life
Is, to my calm sublime, as tropic storm.
When other leech-craft fails the breaking brain,
I, only, own the anodyne to still
Its eddies into visionless repose.
The face, distorted with life's latest pang,
I smoothe, in passing, with an angel wing;
And from beneath the quiet eyelids steal
The hidden glory of the eyes, to give
A new and nobler beauty to the rest.
Belie me not; the plagues that walk the Earth,
The wasting pain, the sudden agony,
Famine, and War, and Pestilence, and all
The terrors that have darkened round my name,
These are the works of Life, they are not mine;
Vex when I tarry, vanish when I come,
Instantly melting into perfect peace,
As at His word, whose master-spirit I am,
The troubled waters slept on Galilee.

Tender I am, not cruel: when I take
The shape most hard to human eyes, and pluck
The little baby-blossom yet unblown,
'Tis but to graft it on a kindlier stem,
And, leaping o'er the perilous years of growth,
Unswept of sorrow, and unscathed of wrong,
Clothe it at once with rich maturity.
'Tis I that give a soul to memory;
For round the follies of the bad I throw
The mantle of a kind forgetfulness;
But, canonised in dear Love's calendar,
I sanctify the good for evermore.
Miscall me not! my generous fulness lends
Home to the homeless, to the friendless friends;
To the starved babe, the mother's tender breast;
Wealth to the poor, and to the restless—rest!

Shall I unveil, Thordisa? If I do,
Then shall I melt at once the iron bonds
Of this mortality that fetters thee.
Gently, so gently, like a tired child,
Will I enfold thee. But thou may'st not look
Upon my face, and stay. In the busy haunts
Of human life, in the temple and the street,
And when the blood runs fullest in the veins,
Unseen, undreamed of, I am often by,
Divided from the giant in his strength
But by the thickness of this misty veil.
But none can look behind that veil, and stay.
Shall I withdraw it now?

Tho.   A little while!
Give me a little yet! Spirit, I love him
And would not go till I have heard once more
In accents whose rich music was the tune
To which my life was set, not that he loves me,
But that he loved me once.   Spirit, not yet!
I am all too earthly in my thoughts of him;
I am not fit for——
Pilgrim.   Hush!   Miscall me not!

[*The* Spirit *disappears*; Thordisa *remains prostrate.*

Enter Gerda.

Ger.   Mistress, where are you?
Tho.   Gerda, come away!
I have much to say; I cannot tell it here.
Tread softly! look not! speak not!   Come away!

[Thordisa *remains looking backward to the place where the* Spirit *stood.*

CHANT IN THE CHAPEL.

Death here is lord of all!
Spread we the funeral pall,
   Hoping, not sighing!
In the far land where rest
Those whom God loves the best,
   There is no dying.

THE CURTAIN FALLS.

ACT III.

SCENE.—*The same. Evening. Horns heard.*

Enter HUGO, SIGURD, LEOFRIC, *and* FRIOTH.

HUGO. A goodly capture, and a goodly day!
    Where is our host, that he breaks faith with us,
    And will not share in the sport?
LEO.   Faith, 'tis his loss.
    He is the foremost hunter of us all,
    And makes me feel a bungler at his side.
FRI. (*to* LEOFRIC). I fancy that he's hunting somewhere else,
    And means to run *his* game down for himself.
LEO. (*to* FRIOTH). Ah, but his oath?
FRI. (*to* LEOFRIC).   Oath! pshaw! a drunkard's vow!
    When was it that he swore? A month ago!
    What was it that he swore? I quite forget!
    It is the noble privilege of wine
    To give full license to our memories
    To play us fast and loose as best we please.

        To take a joke in earnest is a thing
        Which makes a man bad company for his kind.
SIG.   I am ashamed, Sir Hugo, of our host;
        But he lacks breeding.
HUGO.   No, you do him wrong;
        He is a right good gentleman at heart.
        Our courtly polish lends a fair outside,
        But often rubs away the sterling worth,
        Which is too rough of mould to take it well.
SIG. (*aside*). Has he turned coward? Is he shrinking still
        From his sworn purpose, that but now his hand
        Was armed to work on? Or has Isabelle
        Drugged all his senses into impotence?
        A curse upon a woman's apron-strings!
        Their knots are far too intricate to play with.
HUGO. Here comes the laggard, and my wife!
FRI. (*to* LEOFRIC).   You see!
        He brings his bag with him.

           Enter HAROLD *and* ISABELLE.

ISA.   Returned at last!
(*Aside*). Thank Heaven for this!
                        [*She goes to* HUGO.
HAR. (*aside*).   She seeks her husband's side!
        Has she been fooling me?
SIG. (*to* HAROLD).   Where have you been?
        Have you forgot again?
HAR. (*to* SIGURD).   I shall forget
        Just what I please, and when!

SIG. (*aside*). Nay, then, by Heaven
　　I'll shame him to the proof! I will tell Hugo
　　His wife is wanton, and call up the devil
　　Of jealousy to aid me!

HUGO (*to* ISABELLE). Isabelle,
　　Why do you tremble so?

ISA. (*to* HUGO). Oh, my dear lord,
　　If you but knew how I have looked for you!
　　My eyes are happy in your safe return.

HUGO (*to* ISABELLE). My safe return! Am I so poor a hunter
　　That you fear danger for me?

ISA. (*to* HUGO). Yes, I do!
　　I would we were far hence, with all my heart!

HUGO (*to* ISABELLE). You were not wont to be so fearful,
　　child.

SIG. (*aside*). The lover and the husband! rare dissembler!
　　Why, what a brazen thing a woman is!

HAR. (*aside*). She hangs about his neck! her lips are his—
　　Only her promises are mine! (*to* ISABELLE). Take
　　care;
　　The price you offered must be paid in full.

HUGO. Lord Harold, answer for this trembler here.
　　What have you said to her?

SIG. (*aside*). Ay, tell him that!
　　And if you don't, I will, before to-morrow!

ISA. (*aside*). I dare not tell him! Did I breathe the
　　truth,
　　Then my lord's life were forfeited indeed.
　　Would Rolf but tell me all!—My noble husband,

He has been speaking of strange things to me;
Whispering wild tales of witchcraft.

Hugo.   Is that all?
We'll match them with some legends of our own
Over the wine-cup.

Fri.   Come to it at once, then!
I am as dry as a bookworm!

Enter Rolf *from the Castle.*

Rolf.   My Lord Harold,
The supper waits.

Fri.   Oh, blessèd messenger!
Be all your sins forgiven you for those words!
Harold, my Harold, you were slack in the chase,
And if you have not gained an appetite,
I'll eat for both of us—and drink, if need be,
For all the party!

Har.   Gentlemen, come in.
Fair lady, will you grace us with your presence,
As is your wont?

Isa. (*to* Harold).   Spare me your witchcraft, then.

Har. (*to her*). You have not spared me yours.

Fri.   Make haste, make haste.

[*Exeunt into the Castle all but* Sigurd *and* Rolf, *the former stopping the latter as he is following.*

Sig. A word with you. Is it your doing, knave,
That the strong wings of opportunity
Flit thus unheeded by, when we should clip

        And chain them to our uses? Have you come
        Again between this Norman and his fate,
        And with your scruples cooled your master's courage,
        As water drenches wine? You love him not, then?

ROLF. I love him better than I love my life,
        Better than all the world (except, perhaps,
        One foolish little woman, whom I miss
        More than discretion). 'Tis you love him not,
        But only love your malice and yourself!
        Why do you hate the Norman?

SIG.   For his youth
        And for his fairness, as I hate the world,
        The light, and whatsoever power it is
        That brings men such as I am into being,
        And vents its spite on me, who will give back
        As much—and more. For I have but the space
        Of a short life to circumscribe my spleen,
        While it may fashion others like to me,
        And spit its venom out to the end of time.
        I love that boy, though—or I think I do—
        And he shall keep his word; I know a spell
        To set those two at one another's throats.

        [*Going in,* ROLF *stands between him and the door.*

ROLF. You shall not say it, then!
SIG. (*advancing*).   Ha!

            Enter GERDA.

GER.   Rolf!

ROLF.   Who is that?
　　Gerda! Now all goes well, all must go well,
　　　Gerda, my life, my angel!   [*Crosses to her.*
GER.   Touch me not,
　　Thou worthy slave of an unworthy lord!
SIG. (*aside*). Well done, propitious stars! I called upon
　　　The devil of jealousy, and he sends me here
　　　His own familiar.   [*He stops behind and listens.*
ROLF.   Why, what have I done?
GER. Oh, *I* don't know. *You* best can answer that.
ROLF. I'll tell you everything.
GER.   No. Such a tale
　　Were little fitted for a maiden's ear.
　　Oh, you abominably wicked man!
　　Faith-breaker, light-o'-love, pagan!
ROLF.   That's enough!
　　Such ugly words ill suit such pretty lips.
GER. How *dare* you pay a compliment to me?
ROLF. I couldn't help it, and I never can.
GER. You never spoke a truer word than that.
　　Little you care to whom you pay them, though;
　　You offer them, you know, with such a grace,
　　So prettily, so daintily, so——Ah!
　　My very fingers tingle to the tips
　　To think of all the hussies you've been courting
　　In the same language that you talked to me!
　　Little you care for *that*, though, I suppose;
　　All women are alike, sir, are they not,
　　Mere pegs to hang a compliment upon?

ROLF. All women like? Well, if they talk like that,
      I hope they are not, for the sake of men.
      And as for pegs, pray Heaven that some of them
      Abide more quietly in their holes than you,
      Nor creak so harshly.

GER.   *Oh*, how *dare* you come
      Here to insult me?

ROLF.   Gerda! I declare
      This is too much.

GER.   Too much, am I? No doubt,
      You've had enough without me. Have I lived
      To hear I am "too much!"

ROLF.   Not *you*—not *you*.
      I didn't say so.

GER.   But you thought it, sir.
      I saw you think it, and I see you now.

ROLF. You don't.

GER.   I do.

ROLF.   You can't, for no such thought
      Was in my mind.

GER.   Your mind! I dare say not.
      I know that I can see farther than most,
      But not even I can look into your mind,
      Because it isn't there to look into.

SIG. (*aside*). Now, this is very meat and drink to me.

ROLF. Hear me!

GER.   Good heavens! how you interrupt!
      Haven't I heard you quietly all this time?

ROLF. Oh! have you finished?

GER.   Finished—no, indeed!
I've scarcely yet begun.
ROLF (*gloomily*). Then I believe
I shall not be alive to hear the end.
GER. So much the better for the female sex.
SIG. (*aside*). And with this sort of goods men fall in love.
(*Coming forward*). Good even, gentle creature!
GER.   Who are you?
Lord Sigurd?
ROLF.   I forgot him. (*To* GERDA). He has heard
All you've been saying.
GER. (*to* ROLF).   All *you* said to *me*
Is more to the purpose; what he thinks of *you*
I can't imagine; *me* you heard him call
A gentle creature.
ROLF (*to* GERDA).   That was irony.
GER. Don't let him try his "irony" with me,
I'll not endure it. Pardon me, my lord,
(*quieting herself*) I am not smooth enough in speech
for you,
But come as fair Thordisa's messenger.
SIG. And speak in fair Thordisa's gracious tones.
ROLF (*to* GERDA). That's irony again.
GER. (*to* ROLF).   Then I will match him
With his own weapons. Oh, my courteous lord,
My handsome, kind Lord Sigurd, I am come
To Harold, from Thordisa! We have heard
Much of his Norman visitors—his fine lady
And—all her women.

ROLF.   On my life and love,
  There's not a woman with her! Is that all
  That made you jealous?
GER.   *Jealous!* what, of *you*?
  How *dare* you call me jealous?
ROLF.   If you're not,
  I don't know what a woman is.
GER.   Indeed!
  You ought to, by this time.
ROLF.   Again, I swear
  There's but one woman here!
GER.   A harem of them!
  I've heard about your dainty Southern dames;
  They want six maids to put their hair in curl,
  As many more to take it out again;
  Some fan them when they're hot, more fan the fire
  When they are cold—a harem, sir, I swear!
ROLF. Lord Sigurd, tell her that I speak the truth.
SIG. She'd not believe me.
GER.   Very likely not.
  When I believed his promises, I believed
  A man just once too often. They are made
  All of the self-same kidney. Where is Harold?
  What are my wrongs to my lady's? Where is he?
  That I may ask him in whose ear he whispered
  Here, in this place, a few short hours ago,
  The very words with which he won the heart
  That he has broken. Oh, how *could* he do it?
SIG. And—those words were?

Ger.   Thro' Life to Death—thro' Death
To Life!

Sig.   Indeed, a very pretty text!
Thank you—*I'll* ask him.

Rolf.   Mischief! I forgot.

[*Going to the door.* Sigurd *passes before him mockingly, and on the threshold crosses* Isabelle, *who enters from the Castle. He bows to her and goes in.*

Isa.   Hist! Rolf, where are you?

Ger. (*starting*).   There, I told you so.
One of your women wants you.

Rolf.   Gerda, hush!

Ger.   Why should I hush? I shan't!

Rolf.   This is the lady
Of whom you spoke just now—

Isa.   Where are you, Rolf?
Come here to me; I have no friend but you.

Ger.   Oh, you abandoned person!

Isa. (*with dignity*).   This to me?
Who are you? You mistake.

Ger. (*looking at her*).   I think I do.
Your face is gentle, but why are you here?
Are you that Norman that has stolen away
A false heart from Thordisa?

Isa.   I know not
Of whom you speak, nor who Thordisa is,
Or you! But you are woman, and I pine

To see a woman's face. I have met with none
Since first I reached this fatal place till now.

ROLF (*to* GERDA). I told you so.

GER. Are you quite sure of that?

ISA. 'Tis Heaven's own truth.

ROLF (*to* GERDA). There!

GER. (*to* ROLF). I forgive you, then,
For all your falsehood and your violence.

ISA. Do not turn from me; be not harsh with me;
Woman ne'er needed woman's counsel more.
Listen! My fears have overmastered me;
I am a stranger on your northern coast,
Save for my husband, friendless and alone!
He has no thought of fear, nor will believe
The dangers that surround us. I know not
Or what they are, or whence! But in all eyes
I read imagined terrors every hour;
I cannot bear it. (*To* ROLF). Make your warnings clear,
And shape the horrors we must cope withal,
Or—I—
[*Fainting.*

GER. Bring water, she has fainted. Quick!
[*Exit* ROLF.

Enter THORDISA.

She has a fair face!

THO. (*coming forward*). Let me look at it;
Yes, a fair face; and fairer far than mine.

GER. It is not true.
THO. He thinks so; that's enough.
And yet—what is there, Gerda, in these lines,
That they should so cross and disfigure mine,
As leave no trace of them?
GER. Ay, what, indeed?
Why, they are poor and pale.
THO. Yes; so they are.
But then the blood has left them for a while;
And when it courses from the heart again,
And in full channel overflows the veins,
Gives redness to the lip, bloom to the cheek,
And lustre to the eye, then you shall see
How tempting ripe she is. What if I stole
Blood from her arm, think you that it would warm
And make me wanton? He might love me then.
GER. Oh, do not speak like that!
THO. No; she is fair.

Re enter ROLF.

ROLF. My lady! oh, my lady! ere she wakes
Give me your counsel; only you can help
My master in his sorest need.
THO. You jest!
I am nothing to your master; here is she
That shall advise him.
ROLF. No; you do him wrong.
You know not in how terrible a strait

You left him when you parted from this place.
I sought you in the morning—you were gone!
That night! that awful night! Do you remember
The legend that I told you, Gerda?

GER.   Ay;
Earl Olaf's vow. I never was so frightened
In all my life.

THO.   I know that legend well.
What of it now?

ROLF.   That very night, my lord,
Goaded by Sigurd past endurance, took,
In all its terrible solemnity,
That oath upon him.

THO. *and* GER.   What?

ROLF.   And scarce had sworn,
Before these Normans came—this woman here
And her brave husband.

THO.   Husband! Yes, go on.

ROLF. The month expires to-morrow. Ere that time,
With his own hand, his own guest he must slay,
Or pay the forfeit.

GER.   Ah!

THO.   Be still; she wakes!

ISA. (*recovering herself*).
Where am I? Was I dreaming? Did I see
A woman's face just now? (*Seeing* THORDISA.) It
   was not yours.
Hugo!

THO.   Fear nothing for him.

Isa.   What are you
That are so sad and stern, and yet so sweet?
I dread you, yet I trust you. Oh, your eyes
Have all the depth of Heaven in their blue,
And all its truth; and you are very fair.

Tho. Do you think so?

Isa.   Yes.

Tho.   You are no scholar, then,
And read to little purpose. Let your glass
Tell you what beauty is, or what men think
That beauty should be. Gerda, you and Rolf
Take charge of her, and lead her to my house.

Isa. Your house?

Tho.   You wonder? Well, perhaps you might
If you knew all. But doubtless you have heard
Lord Harold speak of a poor slighted thing,
A woman called Thordisa?

Isa.   No.

Tho.   Indeed!
That's passing strange. But now, go to my house,
You will be safe from danger there—not here.

Isa. My husband——

Tho.   Do you love him?

Isa.   From my heart!

Tho. Then what of Harold?

Isa.   He is but a boy.
I did but sport with him, and he with me.

Tho. Sport! I can bear no more! Take her away!

	I answer for your husband. Ere the morning
	He shall be safe with you. Oh, do not touch me!
Isa.	I cannot understand you. I have done
	No wrong to any; there's some error here.
	You will not save my husband?
Tho.	I have said
	I can, and will; and you may trust me.
Isa.	Yes;
	I see I can. Heaven bless you!
Tho.	Mock me not!

    [*Exeunt* Isabelle, Gerda, *and* Rolf.

Earl Olaf's vow! What is a vow to him
That he should keep it—he, who swore to me
One short year's fealty one long month ago,
Then, with a lip still wet with kiss of mine,
And in the very words my folly lent him
To snare a woman with, could pawn again
His counterfeit of love yet unredeemed,
And lie his soul away? But then that oath,
Of which Rolf told me? If he break his faith
With me, a woman, penalty is none
For such a trifle; but Earl Olaf's vow!
How runs the legend? If he keep it—murder!
And if he break it—death! Well, what then?
Why, I have seen and spoken with it. Oh,
The ground is holy where thy feet have trod,
Thou mystery of beauty and of love!

Thy silver tones must lead the worst aright,
And teach the falsest, truth. Death! Let it take him.

[*Shouts and sounds of quarrel from within.*

What noise is that? [*She falls back and listens.*

Enter HAROLD, HUGO, SIGURD, LEOFRIC, *and* FRIOTH.

HUGO. By Heaven, I'll have from you
Your answer to this charge! What, play the traitor
To your own guest, that trusted you as fully
As brother trusts to brother! Is it true
That Sigurd hints?

SIG. Nay, nay, I hinted nothing.
Be gentle with him, Harold; he has drunk
Too much for wisdom. Good Sir Hugo, see,
Harold is mad with wine—it were not well
To press him now.

HAR. I will not talk with you
While you are heated thus.

HUGO. I say you shall.

SIG. Oh, that my innocent words should work such ill!
It was a jest, Sir Hugo, but a jest!
Thro' Life to Death, thro' Death to Life! a pledge
Of little meaning! I but bade you ask him
To whom he gave it——

HUGO. He shall answer that.
Does he speak truly? Did you say those words
To a woman—here—but now?

SIG. (*aside*). It works, it works!
  Let me against each other arm those two,
  And I will look to it which of them shall fall.
HUGO. Answer him, answer! Did you speak those words?
HAR. Yes, I did speak them. Fall my sins on me
  And all who cross me. I did speak those words,
  And I will answer for them with my life,
  My life, or yours! There is no man in the world
  That shall dare question me!
HUGO. Before all here,
  In full arraignment, you shall plead to this:
  To whom were those words spoken? Say, to whom,
  And damn thyself!
THO. (*coming forward*). He spoke those words to me.

THE CURTAIN FALLS.

A lapse of Twenty-four Hours.

ACT IV.

SCENE.—*The same. Night. A Storm raging.* SIGURD *discovered alone.*

SIG.   Forsworn, forsworn! within an hour, forsworn!
Unless the spiteful pilot of the world,
Who laughs to see men sorry, should bethink him
Of that same silken-favoured Norman there,
As a fair freight worth wrecking in its prime,
And blasting into everlasting waste,
Just when it promises best. Why, when I die,
I needs must have some share i' the government
Of mortal business, for it goes almost
As cross as I would rule it.

Enter ROLF.

Well, what news?
What does your master? Does he know the hour?
ROLF. He sits and watches time as it goes by;
And ever as the last sands leave the glass,
And mark another footprint on the day,

THE WHITE PILGRIM.

    He moves his lips and mutters to himself
    Something I cannot hear.
SIG.   He has been thus
    All the day long?
ROLF.   All the long night and day,
    Since he beheld Thordisa, has he sate
    Locked in his turret, all access denied,
    Save to me only; and on me he looks
    As upon nothing—sees me, knows me not.
SIG. Has he not spoken?
ROLF.   No; though once or twice
    I thought he named Thordisa.
SIG.   Let her come
    And look upon her work. Now, but for her,
    Last night had ended all; but since she came,
    And cast the icy shadow of her presence
    Upon the face of the sun, I might as well
    Move yon dull rock to strike the insolent waves
    That chatter at its base, as wake in him
    The spirit of his fathers. Ay, howl on!
    Nature herself is up in arms to-night,
    In censure of our paltering, and the Spirit
    Of Death rides forth upon the wings o' the storm
    To claim the craven who invoked him here,
    And dares not stand the challenge.
ROLF.   What a flash!
    Methought it showed me that white form again,
    Waiting for Harold. What a slave was I
    To stay his hand! I should have armed it here

In triple steel against the Norman stranger,
Who were more fit to die to spare an ache
To Harold's finger, than my lord to fall
For all the blood that waters Normandy!
There may be time——

Sig.   Too late! The spell is on him,
Which none may loose but the fell witch that wove it.
Send his Thordisa here.

Enter THORDISA.

Tho.   Who speaks of me?
Lord Harold's evil spirit?

Sig.   Oh, fair creature,
I would not claim precedence of yourself;
But 'tis no time to bandy courtesies.
Do you love Harold?

Tho.   If you love him, no.

Sig. Say that I love him not, then. Only think
That every storm-driven minute, as it goes,
Is heavy with his life, and bid him hasten
To keep the oath he swore.

Tho.   Bid Harold come,
If my poor name has yet the charm to draw him
To a brief converse. Do not answer. Go!

                             [*Exit* ROLF.

Sig. His life is in your hands; oh, think of that!
A word from you will steel the nerveless heart—
A look from you will fire the frozen spirit.

         Could I but rob you of the power you own
         To move him to your wishes, I would kill you
         Here where you stand, in your pale saintliness,
         And think the deed well done.
THO.   I ask no better:
         It is not good to live.
SIG.   'Tis ill to die.
THO.   Yes; to die ill is ill; but to die well
         Is better than the best.
SIG.   Tell Hugo that;
         And do not rob him of so great a boon.
         For me, I am not enough in love with death,
         To court it for myself, or for my boy.
         What will you say to him?
THO.   Leave that to me.
SIG.   I cannot read the purpose of your heart
         In that cold eye of yours. But mark me, woman!
         If that harm comes to Harold, you shall rue it,
         For I will kill you.
THO.   Pagan! to your knees!
         And pray the Heaven, whose stern arrest you dread,
         To strike at others, but to spare you yet
         For late remorse—repentance—sorrow—shame!
         Talk you of killing—you, whose every word
         Might kill the one immortal part in you,
         But that it *is* immortal, which should make
         Even of that crooked form a thing more fair
         Than the dead glories of the universe?
         Thou, that hast lived for evil from thy birth,

                                                      F

Thou, that in very wantonness of ill
Hast laid this bitter sin on Harold's soul,
On Harold's whom thou lovest ! *lovest—thou !*
Thou, that hast perjured him, and widowed me ;
Thou, that hast blighted man, and outraged God,
Look on the ruin round thee—'tis thy work !

Enter HAROLD.

SIG. Harold !
HAR. Go in ; this is no place for you,
For where she is is Heaven ; go forth from it.

[SIGURD *shrinks off.*

You sent for me?
THO. Yes.
HAR. Why?
THO. To look on you,
And bid you look on me. Are you afraid ?
Is this the Harold whom I knew erewhile ?
Oh, no ; for he was weak, perchance, and yielding,
But he was fearless. In his eyes there shone
A light that made a halo where he went,
And stamped him noble in his own despite.
Where is that lustre now ? And where is he ?
This Harold is not Harold.
HAR. If you will,
Stab me with sharp reproaches ; on my head
Pour all the words of love I spoke to you,
Transmuted into gall ; and let thine eyes,
Changed more than mine, flash anger back on me,

Which once had gathered all the light of love
Into their magic circle. Do all this,
But do not stand thus cold and passionless,
As is the marble to the craftsman's hand,
When he has lost his cunning, and no more
Can fashion life out of the sleeping stone!

THO. Artist, you wrong yourself! Good sooth, you do!
I am not marble, but poor common earth,
That served as matter for your 'prentice hand
To mould in plastic shapes, then throw away
For work more worthy. Oh, your cunning, sir,
Has grown with practice, and your latest model
Has been more deftly carved of fairer stuff.
She sent me to you.

HAR.   Who?

THO.   Have you forgotten
Her name so soon? She is called Isabelle,
And asks you for her husband.

HAR.   You know all?
That I am bound within this hour to kill him,
Or pay the forfeit with my life?

THO.   I know.

HAR. And you would have me—

THO.   Pay it!

HAR.   And be perjured!

THO. Is perjury to you so hard a thing?

HAR. And is my death so slight a thing to thee?

THO. Lighter than such dishonour. Oh, this deed
Would top dishonour, and would underwrite

My griefs against thee with so black a charge,
That Mercy's self must scorn to plead for thee
Before the bar of Justice. Not for me,
That have no longer right or part in you,
But for your soul's sake, stay your hand to-night,
And let the Norman go.

HAR.   I had no soul,
Save that thou lentest me. I'll not stay my hand
For such a scruple. Ask for thine own sake
All that thou wilt. I'll do or leave undone
Anything, everything—so thou wilt plead
As thou wert wont to do.

THO.   Oh, shame upon you!
Do you not hear the wrath of God cry out
Upon your sacrilege? Do you not see
God's eye dart forth the flame to burn you up,
Where self-attainted in his sight you stand?
I will not plead with you as was my wont,
Lest, as your wont was, you should lie to me!
But I will beg the name of Isabelle;
And, being Isabelle, to whom you swore,
But yesterday, a truth beyond the grave,
I say to you, be true but for an hour,
And give me back my husband!

HAR.   And I answer,
I will not. If I love you, Isabelle,—
You, Isabelle, loving me—what offering
Can do such grace to us and to our love,
As this your husband's blood? What blow can rivet

Closer the links of our unhallowed chain,
Than that which strikes him down?

THO.   She loves you not,
Vain-glorious boy! Think you all women are
As weak as I, as easily wooed and won?
With ear so ill-attuned to the rich ring
Of sterling metal, as to take the dross
For the pure ore, the burnished lead for gold,
The churl for the knight, the lackey for the lord?
She loves you not, I say! She played with you,
As, had I courtly breeding, I had played,
Poor puppet in her strings of fairy silk!
And as thy sin, so is thy punishment!

HAR. Was that her message? Give her mine again.
Tell her, my love was counterfeit as hers,
Tell her, my passion grew but of my pain,
And that one sin gave monstrous birth to another,
Worse than itself! I read but in her eyes
The record of mine oath, that oath which damned me
Past all redemption of thy love and thee!
She was the phantom of thy beauty, dear!
I sought in her forgetfulness of thee,
But still thy shadow overshadowed all
Her ripe reality, and made the substance
Seem but the seeming; when I pressed her hardest
With my hot words, it was thy breath that fired them,
Even with the shame it ever cried on me!
Tell her I love her not! Tell her I ask
Her pity and her pardon! Tell her I have

One love—one life—one hope—one saviour—
All called Thordisa. Do not turn away!
What's Hugo now to us? or Isabelle?
Come back to me, come back; I love you so,
That I must wipe my sins out with that love,
Had they ten times their burden. Answer me!

THO. What can I answer?
HAR.   Kiss me!
THO.   Never, never!
What, are you tired of the new toy already,
And would have back the old? Too late, my lord!
Not all the encircling air shall breathe again
Into the frozen ashes one brief spark;
Or, if it seem to do so, it shall be
Like will-o'-the-wisp upon a barren moor,
To lure you to your death!

HAR.   Your words are cruel;
I do not know Thordisa.
THO.   I myself
Now know myself no longer. Oh, the sin,
To change a nature that was soft and kind,
To such a thing as thou hast made of me!
HAR. Thordisa, listen!
THO.   No; between us two
The words of that troth-plight are as a bar
Words cannot overleap. Let Hugo go!
And in His sovereign mercy may the Lord,
Whose face thy guilt has covered, hold His hand,
And spare you to repent. Ay, and me, too;

THE WHITE PILGRIM.

    For I had all forgot Him in my wrongs,
    And He is angry (*muttered thunder*). Do you hear
        Him? Hark!
    It is our sentence.

HAR.   Let me meet it, then,
    As a man should. The ways of Him you pray to
    Are dark to such as I, and I am lost
    In their strange mazes. If, forsworn to thee,
    I must for thee forswear myself again,
    Why, I will do it! What you ask of me
    Is Hugo's life, and what you ask I give,
    Come what come may; but if I fall for him,
    First he shall know the truth, and on his sword
    I'll pay the forfeit of my broken vow,
    And blot dishonour out! Hugo!

          Enter SIGURD.

SIG.   Too late!
    Some juggling devil has been here at work.
    Hugo has fled.

HAR.   Fled?

SIG.   How or where I know not.
    But he has gone: and even now the hour
    Draws to its fatal ending. Who has been
    Hell's messenger to him? Who warned him?

THO.   I!

SIG.   The Christian witch again! nay, then all's lost!

THO.   All's won, all's gained, if Heaven but gain a soul!
    I dared not hope that my weak voice could win

            The boon I asked for. For your sake, not his,
            I wrestled for his life; for with the morning
            He left the castle. He and Isabelle
            Are far away ere this.
HAR.   I am dishonoured,
            And you have done it. Are we even now?
SIG.   We will be, traitress. (*To* HAROLD). Now you know
              the worth
            Of her that has ensnared you. Gone, those two,
            To make a sport of the northern savages
            Among their courtly minions.
HAR.   Gone!

               Enter HUGO.
HUGO.   Not yet.
HAR. Ah!
SIG. (*to* HAROLD). There is time; kill him!
THO.   Oh, God, have mercy!

   [HUGO *and* HAROLD *face each other with drawn swords.*

HUGO. I have learned all, young sir, from Isabelle.
         I will not call you knight; for in my country
         The man who thus, under his own roof-tree,
         Plots 'gainst the life and honour of his guest,
         And masks the face of murder and of lust
         With the fair-seeming smile of fellowship,
         If such a thing could live, must strike the spurs
         With his own base hand from his serpent heel,
         Ere dare to wear them! Oh, that one so young
         Should be so old a villain! Think you, sir,

    That I would leave this coast infested thus,
    Nor strive to rid it, first, of such as thou !
    Defend yourself.
THO.   Oh, spare him !
HUGO.   Gentle lady,
    I saw you not. If you will go with us,
    My Isabelle shall tend you as a sister,
    For your kind service.
THO.   For that service, spare him !
HUGO. You are too true a woman not to know
    A true man's sacred duty. For my wife
    And for my honour. Leave us, I entreat.
SIG. (*to* THORDISA). Stand by, and watch the issue of your
    love.
THO. What have I done? Where are you, Isabelle ?
              [*Exit.*

SIG. (*aside*). Now then, my trusty counsellor !

        [*Half drawing his sword.*

HUGO.   To your guard.
HAR. I will not fight with you.
HUGO.   What ?
HAR.   You have spoken
    The truth, and less. Yes, I have been most base ;
    Base and unknightly. Yes, I swore to kill you,
    And would have done it. Yes, I would have made
    Your wife my mistress. But all this is nothing
    In my great sum of sin ; for from my brow
    I plucked the brightest jewel of the earth

And trod it in the mire. Thordisa's love
I had, and lost. Look on my sword, Sir Hugo;
As keen and shining was my honour once,
As smooth and fair my fortune, till one day
I broke them—thus. (*Breaking his sword*). Kill me;
   it is your right. [*He folds his arms across his eyes.*

SIG. Ay, and his duty! Use it, Norman, do;
And let thy hand do justice for us all
On this degenerate puny stripling here,
Who shames all manhood. These be your new creeds,
That teach a man to write himself a cur.
I'll none of them, or you, but I will go
And rail my tongue out 'gainst a world that rears
Nothing but mongrels. I have cared for you,
That do not even care to curse at me
For bringing you to this. Well, peace be with you!
A Christian peace! and may all pagan plagues
Be doubled in that word. Die, fool, and rot!

                                            [*Exit.*

HAR. You see me as I am, a butt for all,
Good men and knaves, to shoot at; and already,
If words could kill the body, as they kill
The heart beyond all surgery, should I lie
Mere carrion at your foot. Why do you wait?

HUGO. I am no executioner, Sir Harold,
Nor you the thing I thought you. On your face
I read an open record fairly writ,
That doth belie your fault. May Heaven forbid
That I should mar its blazon! Boy, you sinned

　　　　But in the thought; and standing self-condemned,
　　　　You stand to me acquit.   Young brother-in-arms,
　　　　I do absolve you freely.   Fail no more!
HAR. Come these words from your heart?
HUGO. 　　　　　　　　　　　　　　'Tis in my hand,
　　　　Take it.
HAR. Ay; with my lips, and on my knee.   [*Kneeling.*

　　　　　Enter THORDISA *and* ISABELLE.

THO. Come with me, come! Oh, lend me strength to plead;
　　　　Lend me thy winning tongue, thy fairy grace,
　　　　Thy mellow wiles, the blush that burns betimes,
　　　　To light up worship.   Come!   I am so weak
　　　　That thought myself so strong in scorn of him,
　　　　That I would rather see him in your arms
　　　　Than at your husband's foot.
ISA. (*smiling*). 　　　　　　　　　Yet he is there.
HUGO. Rise, Harold.   Here is she to whom your knees
　　　　Owe all their fealty.
THO. (*drawing back*). 　　　　Safe!
HUGO. 　　　　　　　　　　　　Come, Isabelle.
(*To* THO.)   Forgive him, lady, he is worth forgiveness.
HAR. (*to* ISABELLE).   First give me yours, fair Norman, and
　　　　　farewell;
　　　　If you should think of me when you are gone,
　　　　Be it as of one who died when he was young,
　　　　And had not learned to live.
ISA. 　　　　　　　　　　　I will think of you
　　　　As of a wayward but a noble heart,

   Kept in such keeping, that its fitful pulse
   Beats with a steadier music day by day,
   Till age steal gently o'er its harmonies,
   And lull them to repose more musical
   Than the best concords of a jarring world.
   Adieu, Sir Pagan! As I think, you know
   The trick of lovers' vows, forget it not!
   You are forgiven. Sister, fare you well!

       [*Exeunt* HUGO *and* ISABELLE.

THO. Farewell! I know not how all this may end;
   But as from yon black storm-cloud breaks the sky,
   So hope shines through thy sin. The tempest's fury
   Is well-nigh spent.
HAR.   There are more clouds behind:
   And even their latest message teems with fires
   That carry death. Look! It is dark again,
   But through their rift the moon showed at the full,
   And the bell treads upon the stroke of one.
   My hour is come, Thordisa. I have broken
   That oath for thee, and I did well to break it.
   But turn thy face in kindness upon mine,
   For I shall never see it any more.
THO. It cannot be!
HAR.   I know it.
THO.   Dreams! And yet
   What change is on thy face! Some unseen hand

　　　　　Writes on its page in fearful characters
　　　　　Something I cannot read.　Come closer to me.
Har.　The unknown language of the land unknown.
　　　　　I soon shall hear it spoken.　Hark! In the air
　　　　　I hear it now.
Tho.　　　　　　　It is the dying storm!
Har.　That shall not die alone.　Thordisa, listen,
　　　　　There is so little time.　I give my life
　　　　　To please you—that is nothing.　Where I go to
　　　　　You say you know—I do not—but it must be
　　　　　Where I shall be a stranger.　Let me take
　　　　　Some gentle record of the place which knew me,
　　　　　To bear me company where I am not known,
　　　　　Or I shall feel so lonely.
Tho.　　　　　　　Hush! oh, hush!
Har.　Ay, soon I shall!　Tell me—when I am gone
　　　　　Into that country, and the trackless hills,
　　　　　Which are its nearest confines, have shut out
　　　　　Earth's real sounds for ever, shall I not
　　　　　Hear for awhile the echo of my life
　　　　　Roll back across them, in the words that last
　　　　　Fell on my living ear?
Tho.　　　　　　　Harold!
Har.　　　　　　　　Oh, yes!
　　　　　That is the sound that I would take with me!
　　　　　I have not heard it for so long—so long!
　　　　　All has been bitter here!　Say that again,
　　　　　Say just my name!　I dare not ask for more!

Tho. But you shall have it! You shall have it all
    That heart can fashion or words imitate,
    For I adore you! I forgive you—no—
    I know that I have nothing to forgive—
    Nothing! It was not you that played me false!
    It was not you that broke your troth to me!
    It was your evil angel, who had drugged
    Your own true self to sleep, and breathed that oath
    Which, like the sudden blast upon the grain,
    Blighted the promise of our harvest time!
    And as it was not you, so shall not you
    Die for the forfeit.
Har.   Love! But now I can.
Tho. You will not be so cruel; do not leave me
    Just when I find you. No, you cannot die,
    Shielded by such a death-proof love as mine!

        The bell strikes one, and the White Pilgrim
        appears. Both pause, chilled and horror-
        stricken. The Pilgrim *advances.*

Har. (*dazed*). I do not know that form.
Tho.   Ah, God, I do!
Har. (*facing the* Pilgrim, *who has come down between them.*
    Thordisa *has fallen back.*)
    Yes, it is coming. I am not afraid.
    Why, this is sleep—no worse. Who art thou, then?
    What is thy message?

PIL.   To the restless—rest!

   [*Unveils to* HAROLD, *who sinks at her feet.*
   THORDISA *springs forward as the veil closes
   again.*

THO. Harold!

HAR.   Why, Death is not so hard as Life.
'Tis better so, belovèd, better so! [*Dies.*

THO. Oh, not alone! Dear Spirit, look on me!
I know my heart is breaking—is it not?
For if it were not, it were worse than stone.
I must go hence; I will not stay behind!
Sweet Spirit, let me not! Unite us now
In the one union we may ever know—
We that so loved each other! Oh, draw back
The envious curtain that enfolds you both,
And let me see the face behind the veil!
(*Triumphantly*). My heart *is* broken!

PIL. (*unveiling to* THORDISA). Like a tired child!

   [THORDISA *sinks down by* HAROLD'S *side.*

THO. Darling, you will not be a stranger there! [*Dies.*

   The figure of the PILGRIM *disappears. Enter*
   SIGURD, LEOFRIC, FRIOTH, ROLF, GERDA,
   *and others with torches, who rush up to
   the figures, then stand awe-struck and silent.*
   GERDA *in* ROLF'S *arms. The music breaks
   out from the Chapel in the hymn which
   closed the Second Act*:

Death here is Lord of all!
Spread we the funeral pall,
 Hoping, not sighing!
In the far land where rest
Those whom God loves the best
 There is no dying.

CURTAIN.

OCCASIONAL POEMS.

G

OCCASIONAL POEMS.

HORACE'S GHOST.

(A DEDICATION.)

GENTLE reader—patron mine—
Born of old and patient line,
Some with eager zest embrace
Glories of the field and chase;
Covet these the athlete's prize,
Guerdon meet in lady's eyes;
Those, Ambition's clarion calls
To the Commons' storied halls,
Heart and Will by Fancy set
On the star and coronet;
Battle some for golden gain,
Garners stored with Indian grain;
Him, the wealth Golconda yields
Tempts not from his father's fields,
On a sea-bound bark to roam
From the safety of his home;

While another courts in vain
Dull repose from wind and main,
Praising Ease—to test anew
Fragile freight and careless crew
Some the wine-cup's vigils keep;
Some in busy daylight sleep
By the crystal fountain's sheen,
Or beneath the covert green;
Blithe the soldier springs to arms,
Vainly Beauty woos and charms,
When the boar and tiger near
Tempt the hunter's gun and spear.
Godlike all our pleasures be,
For the Lords of Earth are we.
Ivied Muse of frolic song,
Set me 'mid thy joyous throng;
Do not all thy smiles deny
To thy constant votary!
Let me win the lowest place
In thy dear and winsome grace;—
Happy then, and passion-free,
Earth has naught to offer me.

OLD AND NEW ROME.

WHAT came we forth to see? a fair or race?
Some hero fêted by an eager crowd?
Or would we do some favoured princeling grace,
That thus we herd so close, and talk so loud?

Pushing and struggling, fighting, crushing, shouting,
What are these motley gazers here to seek,
Like merry-makers on a summer outing?
'Tis but the services of Holy Week.

The Eternal City swarms with eager strangers
From every quarter of the busy earth;
Who fill the temples like the money-changers,
And say some prayers—for what they may be worth.

In never-ending tide of restless motion,
They come to burn, in fashion rather odd,
The incense of their polyglot devotion,
Before the altars of the Latin God.

As flock the Londoners to Epsom Races,
Or form a "queue" to see the newest play,
So do the pilgrim-tourists fight for places
Before the chapels in their zeal to pray.

From holy place to holy place they flit,
To "do" as many churches as they can;
And humbly kneeling, for the fun of it,
They climb the ladder of the Lateran.

Here some fair maid, her Heavenward journey steering,
Where by Swiss bayonets the way is barred,
Nor Law, nor Pope, nor Antonelli fearing—
Breaks through the lines of the astonished guard.

In customary suit of solemn black,
With string of beads and veil *à l'Espagnole*,
She means to "see it all;" to keep her back
Would be to peril her immortal soul.

There a slim youth, while all but he are kneeling,
Through levelled opera-glass looks down on them,
When round the Sistine's pictured roof is pealing
Our buried Lord's majestic Requiem.

For him each storied wonder of the globe is
" The sort of thing a fellow ought to see;"
And so he patronised *Ora pro nobis*,
And wanted to encore the *Tenebræ*.

Stranger! what though these sounds and sights be grandest
Of all that on Earth's surface can be found?
Remember that the place whereon thou standest,
Be thy creed what it may, is holy ground.

Yet I have gaped and worshipped with the rest—
I, too, beneath St. Peter's lofty dome
Have seen, in all their richest colours dressed,
The golden glories of historic Rome;

Have heard the Pontiff's ringing voice bestow,
'Mid cheering multitudes and flags unfurled,
Borne by the cannon of St. Angelo,
His blessing on the " City and the World;"

Have seen—and thrilled with wonder as I gazed—
Ablaze with living lines of golden light,
Like some fire-throne to the Eternal raised,
The great Basilica burn through the night;

Have heard the trumpet-notes of Easter Day,
Their silver echoes circling all around,
In strange unearthly music float away,
Stones on the lake translated into sound;—

Yet would I wander from the crowd apart,
While heads were bowed and tuneful voices sang,
And through the deep recesses of my heart
A still small voice in solemn warning rang.

"Oh vanity of vanities! ye seem,
Ye pomps and panoplies of mortal state,
To make this text the matter of your theme,
That God is little, and that Man is great.

"Is this parade of the world's wealth and splendour
The lesson of the simple Gospel-word?
Is this the sacrifice of self-surrender
Taught by the lowly followers of the Lord?

"Do we, who broider thus the garment's hem,
Think of the swaddling-clothes the child had on?
Grace we the casket, to neglect the gem?
Forget we quite the manger for the throne?"

   *   *   *   *

While thus in moralising mood I pondered,
 I turned me from the hum of men alone;
And, as my vagrant fancy led me, wandered
 Amid the maze of monumented stone.

The crowd their favourite lions now forswore,
 Left galleries and ruins in the lurch;
The cicerone's glory was no more,
 For all the world was gathered in the church

So at my will I strayed from place to place,
   From classic shrines to modern studios—
Now musing spellbound, where Our Lady's* face
   In nameless godhead from the canvas glows.

Now, from the still Campagna's desolate rise,
   I saw the hills with jealous clasp enfold
The lingering sunlight, while the seaward skies
   Paled slowly round the melting disc of gold;

Now gazed, ere yet on dome and tower had died
   The glory of the Roman afterglow,
Over the map-like city lying wide,
   Half-dreaming, from the Monte Mario.

Traveller, do thou the like; and wouldst thou learn
   How Rome her faithful votaries enthralls
With all the memories that breathe and burn
   Within the magic circle of her walls,

Leave pomp of man and track of guide-led tourist,
   And drink of history at the fountain-head;
For living minds and living things are poorest
   In that vast mausoleum of the dead.

There, where the stately Barberini pile
   Like some new Nimrod's fabric heav'nward climbs,
Enduring monument of Christian guile,
   By outrage wrested from the Pagan times; †

---

* The Madonna of Foligno.
† "Quod non fecerunt barbari, fecerunt Barberini."

Where lulled and drowsy with the distant hum,
 The sentinel keeps watch upon the town,
And from the heights of old Janiculum
 On Father Tiber's yellow face looks down;

Where in their southern grace the moonbeams play
 On Caracalla's tesselated floors,
And rescue from the garish light of day
 The Colosseum's ghostly corridors;

Where Raphael and all his great compeers
 Art's form divine in giant-mould have cast,
The very air is heavy with the years,
 The very stones are vocal of the past.

Still, as we saunter down the crowded street,
 On our own thoughts intent, and plans, and pleasures,
For miles and miles, beneath our idle feet,
 Rome buries from the day yet unknown treasures.

The whole world's alphabet, in every line
 Some stirring page of history she recalls;
Her Alpha is the Prison Mamertine,
 Her Omega, St. Paul's without the Walls.

Above, beneath, around, she weaves her spells,
 And ruder hands unweave them all in vain:
Who once within her fascination dwells,
 Leaves her with but one thought—to come again.

OLD AND NEW ROME.

So cast thine obol into Trevi's fountain—
  Drink of its waters—and, returning home,
Pray that by land or sea, by lake or mountain,
  " All roads alike may lead at last to Rome."

Easter, 1869.

THE WISHES OF A DUMB-WAITER.*

To circle round the "social board,"
   'Mid wit and wine, I am not able;
Nor, with rich fruits and dainties stored,
   To wait upon your dinner-table.

Domestic in my tastes and ways,
   On humbler errand am I come;
The breakfast-hour my gifts displays,
   The servant of a quiet home.

Of my new masters I've no fears;
   For he, who recommends the place,
Has known the worth of one for years,
   And reads the other's—in her face.

And so, a willing drudge, I'll turn
   Upon my rounds without ado,
And wonder at the hissing urn
   For waiting noisily on you.

     * Given as a present upon a wedding-day.

THE WISHES OF A DUMB-WAITER.

Centre of gravity sedate,
   I watch o'er household griefs and blisses,
But hold my tongue, and never prate
   Either of quarrels or of kisses.

Like some good commonplace M.P.,
   I to my betters "pass the butter;"
And, in my way as wise as he,
   Turn round and round, but never utter.

My trusty counsel I can keep
   Whene'er my lady has the vapours;
Or, fidgety from want of sleep,
   My master d——s the morning papers.

But happier, that I never tire
   Of listening to the cozy chat
And simmer by the new-lit fire—
   The pleasant talk of this and that—

The morning's plan for work or play—
   The homely cares—the homely joys—
And, on the welcome holiday,
   The laughter of the girls and boys.

The choicest blessings of the hearth
   For you, through me, the sender prays,
With all the good things upon earth,
   As health, and wealth, and length of days.

Long may the " whirligig of time "
   For you lay its "revenges" by,
And point the moral of my rhyme,
   By turning smoothly, as will I.

God speed you then : *locutus sum*,
   And, having once the silence broken,
I shall for evermore be dumb :
   Excuse me, please, for having spoken.

LADY FAIR.

UNDERNEATH the beech-tree sitting,
With that everlasting knitting,
And the soft sun-shadows flitting
    Through your wavy hair;
All my thoughts and plans confusing,
All my resolution loosing,
Say, what matter's in your musing,
    Lady fair?

Oh, the charm that in your face is!
All the loves and all the graces!
To be clasped in your embraces
    Were a monarch's share:
Not a man, I ween, who sees you,
But would give his life to please you,
Yet you say—that lovers tease you!
    Lady fair!

One by one, to their undoing,
Fools in plenty come a-wooing,
Baffled still, but still pursuing,
    Tangled in the snare:
In your ever-changing smile hid,
Or beneath your sleepy eyelid,
Many a heart it hath beguilèd,
    Lady fair!

While the summer breezes fan her
Gently with their leafy banner,
Venus' form and Dian's manner
    Doth my goddess wear;
Lives the man who can discover
Any secret spell to move her
To the wish of mortal lover,
    Cold as fair?

But to see those dark eyes brighten,
And for me with kindness lighten,
While the cheek's rich colours heighten,
    What would I not dare?
To inform their scornful splendour
With the love-light soft and tender,
Bow the proud heart to surrender,
    Lady fair!

By the lives that thou hast broken,
By the words that I have spoken,
By the passion they betoken,
    I have loved, I swear,
Only thee since I have seen thee;
And, if woman's heart be in thee,
I will die, but I will win thee,
    Lady fair!

LA VIOLETTA.

Thou art my loadstar and my queen; to thee
The current of my heart sets ebblessly,
Tho' all unheeded the poor offering be.

The soft twin-lamps that from thy fair face shine,
Lit with a tenderness that's only thine,
Burn ever at my fancy's inmost shrine.

If I might choose my fate, I would entreat
To be a carpet for thy dainty feet,
When I return to that I came from, sweet;

Or to be native to the southern sky,
Which for thy head makes fitting canopy—
A waif upon thy path to live and die.

Now I but ask, for all memorial,
That from thine eyes upon my grave may fall
One crystal drop, to grace my funeral.

And on the tomb, ere yet that dew be dried,
Thus let my life's brief tale be signified—
" He only prayed for her, and stood aside."

Venice, 1870.

LONDON LOVES.*

THE day of parting has come, dear,
  The day we've delay'd so long;
But the strings of my lute are dumb, dear
  And have lost their trick of song.

I have known them the hour together
  Run on to the lightest theme—
The fashions, the parks, or the weather,
  A fancy, a flower, a dream.

When the mirth of life was maddest,
  To my hand they would leap and bound;
And when darkest my mood and saddest,
  Would whisper their softest sound.

Whenever the day was breezy,
  Whenever the mad moon shone,
Rhyme-spinning was just as easy
  As loving,—and passing on.

* Written just before an illness of some years.

LONDON LOVES.

Of the garden of sweet girl-dancers
   If one pleased me more than the rest,
And our hands, as they met in the Lancers,
   For a moment clung and press'd,

Ere the world was another day older,
   I would sing her a song of love
Inscribed to her round white shoulder,
   Or the little pink ear above.

I catalogued in my ditty
   All her charms, with a verse for each,
And vowed that her eyes were witty,
   If her tongue lack'd the gift of speech.

O ye loves, ye loves of London,
   Ye hearts of its women and men,
That are all in a moment undone,
   And sooner mended again!

Ye loves of the loveless sinner,
   Ye loves of the box and the Row,
Loves born with the oysters at dinner,
   And drain'd with the curaçoa!

Loves without ruth or scorning,
   I have worn you fresh and bright
With my boutonnière in the morning,
   To die with its leaves at night.

There's many a pretty person
   With thought-unwrinkled brow
I've hung my garland of verse on,
   Whose name I've forgotten now.

But not to such love-notes only
   Was I wont to tune my lute:
As I willed, in my seasons lonely,
   'Twas vocal for me, or mute.

I loved it well, for it made me
   A kingdom all my own,
Where never a foe could invade me,
   Save a halting verse alone.

But to-day, when I fain would wake it
   To a high and tender strain,
Does the spirit of song forsake it?
   Must I sweep its chords in vain?

Sweetheart, as our voyage is ended,
   A chaplet I'd weave for thee
Of choice thoughts cunningly blended,
   To wear for the love of me.

But my plodding fancy lingers,
   Uncaught by the spark of fire,
And falter my listless fingers
   On the nerves of the broken lyre.

THESPIAN THEMES.

OF all the themes of mortal dreams
   That make your sleep uneasy,
Sure never man had sweeter than
   The form of Clara Vesey!

That shapely limb, with ankle slim,
   A foot no boot can better, a
Neat calf, and knee in symmetry,
   And fairy waist, etcetera,

Across your glance will seem to dance,
   And at your studies tease ye,
And make you swear that never were
   Charms like them, Clara Vesey!

The wealthiest fair in Belgrave Square
   (Or else I little know them),
Would gladly owe a plum or so,
   To have them, and to show them.

The sagest dame of school-board fame,
    Of mind and mien commanding,
Would give her lore and something more,
    For Clara's understanding;

And could it ape that perfect shape
    (Although the thought be shocking),
Would offer to the public view
    The whole of her blue stocking.

The most sedate heads in the State,
    As Cardwell, Selborne, Earl Grey,
Would dazzled be those gems to see,
    So featly cased in pearl-grey.

They cannot shun comparison,
    For sure as eggs men call eggs,
The only rage upon the stage
    Is legs, and legs, and more legs!

They come in hose of pink and rose,
    In black and blue and yellow,
In green and red, and turn the head
    Of many a simple fellow.

There's long, there's short, there's every sort
    Of make that's been since Adam;
Some girls are known to wear their own,
    And some believed to pad 'em.

But well I wot, with pads or not,
  There's ne'er a one of these is
(My style is gone) a "patch" upon
  Enchanting Clara Vesey's.

My pretty page, could I engage
  "Supporters" half so clever,
Oh, I'd behave like Geneviève,*
  And "run" on them for ever.

* The opera of *Geneviève de Brabant*, very popular when this wa written.

ÆTATE XIX.

N<small>INETEEN</small> ! of years a pleasant number ;
    And it were well
If on his post old Time would slumber
    For Isabel :

If he would leave her, fair and girlish,
    Untouched of him,
Forgetting once his fashions churlish,
    Just for a whim !

But no, not he ; ashore, aboard ship,
    Sleep we, or wake,
He lays aside his right of lordship
    For no man's sake ;

But all untiring girds his loins up
    For great and small ;
And as a miser sums his coins up,
    Still counts us all.

ÆTATE XIX.

As jealous as a nine-days' lover,
    He will not spare,
'Spite of the wealth his presses cover,
    One silver hair;

But writes his wrinkles far and near in
    Life's every page,
With ink invisible, made clear in
    The fire of age.

Child! while the treacherous flame yet shines not
    On thy smooth brow,
Where even Envy's eye divines not
    That writing now,

In this brief homily I read you
    There should be found
Some wholesome moral, that might lead you
    To look around,

And think how swift, as sunlight passes
    Into the shade,
The pretty picture in your glass is
    Foredoomed to fade.

But, 'faith, the birthday genius quarrels
    With moral rhyme,
And I was never good at morals
    At any time;

While with ill omens to alarm you
    'Twere vain to try;
To show how little mine should harm you,
    Your mother's by!

And what can Time hurt me, I pray, with,
    If he insures
Such friends to laugh regrets away with
    As you—and yours?

EN PASSANT.

An April sun, a silver wave
That laughs and breaks upon the shore—
Such span to us Dame Fortune gave,
        One week—no more!

Two barques upon the summer-foam,
That meet and greet and part at sea—
One outward bound, and one for home:
        Like them were we.

A flower that blossoms in a day,
And dies even there where it was born—
Such was our story, you may say
        To-morrow morn.

The how, and when, that first we spoke,
I do not, and I would not, know;
Dream-like the mutual fancy woke,
        And perished so.

Yet sometimes, in this world of ours,
The wave will drop a waif behind,
The dream will leave a thought, the flowers
    A scent in mind.

So may of mine abide with you,
As ever shall of yours with me,
A word, a smile, a look or two,
    A memory.

WAKE, ENGLAND, WAKE!

AND thought we that his reign could cease?
    And thought we that his day was done?
For that the gentle hand of Peace
    Had loosed the War-God's fiery zone?
Wake, England, wake! let heart and hand be steady!
Still for thy motto take: Ready—aye ready!

A touch—a flash!—he breaks his chain,
    And starts to new and awful birth,
To loose Hell's husbandmen amain,
    And sow in blood the fallow earth.

This is no time for pride of pelf;
    This is no time to sleep or save:
Britain, arise and arm thyself!
    Peace has no home this side the grave.
Wake, England, wake! let heart and hand be steady!
Still for thy motto take: Ready—aye ready!

Men tell us that our arm is weak;
    Men tell us that our blood is cold;
And that our hearts no longer speak
    With the rich trumpet-note of old.

With threat and taunt, with scoff and sneer,
    They gather round the lion's den,
And deem him all too deaf to hear
    The growing tread of armèd men.
Wake, England wake! let heart and hand be steady!
Still for thy motto take: Ready—aye ready!

Above, around, and east and west,
    The storm-clouds muster swift and dark;
Think we the flood of fire to breast,
    Safe in our isle as in the ark?

The Prussian is at Paris' gates—
    The Prussian dons the iron crown,
And marshals all the vassal States
    That at his mailèd foot bow down.

The Russian crouches for his spring;
    Columbia rails in England's tongue,
And waits to pierce, with mortal sting,
    The mighty loins from which she sprung.
Wake, England, wake! let heart and hand be steady!
Still for thy motto take: Ready—aye ready!

Faint not nor fail, ye sons of those
    Who were the bravest born of men:
Our nearest friends may be our foes
    Ere Christmastide come round again.

Though praying yet for peace on earth,
    Keep dry your powder while you can,
Forearmed to meet for home and hearth
    Man's message of good-will to man.

Pray we that soon on every land,
    The reign of all the saints may come;
But till its dawning, sword in hand
    Await we that millennium.
Wake, England, wake! let heart and hand be steady!
Still for thy motto take: Ready—aye ready!

February, 1871.

THE TWENTY-FOURTH OF MAY.

In blood and fire and vapour of smoke
    Hidden his face, the sun sinks down—
Sun, that the bright May morning woke
    Over a glorious godless town.

The work of the centuries, warp and woof,
    Shrivels to dust in the breath of Hell;
As winged with ruin, from roof to roof,
    Flashes the angel Azraël.

Craven hands find the courage to slay,
    And starvèd bodies the life to bleed:
Justice stands in her hall at bay,
    Hall of the "footsteps lost" indeed.

Memories olden are thrown broadcast
    Here and there on the burning breeze;
Line upon line of the storied past
    Falls with the falling Tuileries.

THE TWENTY-FOURTH OF MAY.

Treasures of old-world art unpriced,
  Circled and hemmed in a flaming ring;
Temples of kings and shrines of Christ:
  What are they that have done this thing?

France! that but one brief year ago
  Stood as Napoleon's column stood,
Towering over the world below,
  Mighty in boastful hardihood,—

France! that riven and rent in twain,
  Prostrate under the pitiless skies,
Fallen as ne'er to rise again,
  Lies as Napoleon's column lies,—

Live we? breathe we? hear we aright?
  Is it a nightmare all men see?
Is there a sun? a world? a light?
  God in Heaven! can these things be?

What are they who have brought to birth
  Sights that their father-fiends appal,
Till even the uttermost ends of earth
  Echo their ghastly carnival?

Was it for this that ye called and cried
  For vengeance meet on the foreign foe?
Was it for this that ye starved and died,
  Women and children, high and low?

Was it for this, that men might tell,
    How, in the face of the Uhlan lance,
Paris, unscathed by the stranger's shell,
    Armed her own sons to murder France?

Sleeps or dreams He, the Lord of Lords?
    Or stands he aloof as the German stands,
Watching the clash of kindred swords,
    With eyes unshrinking, and folded hands?

Goth and Visigoth, Vandal and Hun,
    History's bywords, proverbs of shame,
Never yet did what these have done,
    The People's sons, in the People's name!

    *   *   *   *

1871.

A HOME-SIDE STORY.

She was a fair and sunny child,
   When first I knew her;
Her winning ways my heart beguiled,
   And knit me to her.
World-worn, and tossing on the tide
   And storm of life,
I loved to have her at my side,
   My baby-wife.

On fairy lore her mind I fed,
   And sage romances,
That filled the pretty little head
   With earnest fancies.
While as her gracious childhood grew,
   Shone from her eyes
That wondrous light of wisdom true—
   Than ours more wise—

Which as a lesson grave and good,
   And taught of Heaven,
Through the pure lips of infanthood,
   To man is given.

Drawn daily closer each to each
   In heart we were;
But more than I to her could teach,
   I learned from her.

We parted: I for other climes
   And hard endeavour
To do my battle with the times,
   Which fight us ever.
But, whether Fortune frowned or smiled,
   Still in my mind
I kept the image of the child
   I left behind.

She grew up on the quiet path
   Of homely duty,
In all that mind or body hath
   Of grace and beauty;
'Mid her allotted joys and cares
   Pursued her way,
But still remembered, in her prayers,
   For me to pray.

Formed and compact of sober stuff,
   In simple fashion
My life went on with friends enough,
   But strange to passion.
I thought myself the common lot
   Of earth above;
Light fancies I had known, but not—
   What men call Love.

     *   *   *   *

We met again: the budding flower,
  So fondly tended,
Had borne at its appointed hour,
  A blossom splendid.
Another tale on me had told
  The years that fled,
Which, while they filled my hand with gold,
  Silvered my head.

No need of many words to tell
  How then I met her;
Changed as she was, I knew her well—
  Who could forget her?
About her was some subtle sense
  Of sweet perfume,
That, waiting on her innocence,
  Entered the room.

The world, with all its silken ties,
  Closely had bound her;
The young, the noble, breathed their sighs,
  And vows around her.
Then learned I, from the sudden smart
  Of jealous pain,
That I had found, within my heart,
  My youth again.

I watched, if haply in her eyes
  I might discover,
From wandering glance, or swift surprise,
  The favoured lover.

But she was calm and kind, the while
    Methought was worn
A something, in her friendly smile,
    Of quiet scorn.

I stepped from out the throng: her glance
    Went through and through me,
And gave in wordless utterance,
    Her welcome to me.
Her very start was a caress;
    She did not speak;
But flushed, with sudden tenderness,
    From brow to cheek.

No thought had she of name or fame,
    Of rank or glory;
And soon in faltering accents came
    The old old story.
Her heart's desire was this, to share
    With me her life:
And so I won, and so I wear
    My noble wife.

MDLLE. CROIZETTE IN "THE SPHINX"

IN a town we know
   (And I love it dearly),
Where the painters show
   Pretty pictures yearly,
There was one on view—
   If your thoughts you force back
Just a year or two—
   Of a girl on horseback.

Dainty little dame !
   Neat her waistie's span was ;
And the painter's name
   Carolus Duran was.
Ne'er before had girls
   Such inviting noses,
Teeth so like to pearls,
   Peeping out of roses.

And there shone a light
   In the saucy eye, which
Made you pass the night,
   Dreaming of the sly witch,

Rivals scattering
  In a general set-to,
All the spoils to bring
  Mdlle. Croizette to—

Saying: "I adore
  E'en the chair you sit on;
Have some pity for
  A distracted Briton!
Lived I up a tree,
  Slept I in a barn, it
Would be bliss with thee,
  Comedy incarnate!"

Thus I thought of you,
  Prettiest of minxes!
Is't the same, then, who
  Acting in "The Sphinx" is?
Changing us to stones,
  Chilling all our blood in
All our marrowbones,
  Dying on a sudden?—

Turning hot to cold?
  Thrilling all the pit—ex-
Pecting to be told
  Next day by the critics,
In their ancient song,
  That—it wouldn't do; that
This was much too strong;—
  Nothing very new that.

"Surely as my wife
   Wears another's back-tress,"
Quoth I, "on my life,
   You were born an actress!"
And your graceful form
   While my greedy eyes ate,
Thus my fancy warm
   Rhymed you, pretty Croizette!

Paris, 1874.

"LE SPHINX."

À MADEMOISELLE CROIZETTE.

Quoi ? c'est donc vous ? vous, dont la douce figure
    Me souriait jadis si finement ?
Il n'y a pas là de mal, je vous le jure :
    C'est en photographie, seulement.

Vous que j'aimais si bien—dans la fenêtre—
    Vous que je courtisais—sur le carton—
Vous que j'ai vue à mes yeux reparaître,
    Et à cheval—à l'exposition !

"Trop fort," dit-on ! Ma foi donc, qu'on le dise ;
    N'a pas d'esprit qui veut ; et, quant à celà,
Ce n'est pas tout le monde qui s'avise
    D'être trop fort de cette force là.

Vous arrachez des larmes à la parterre ;
    Et même—écrits en très mauvais Français—
Ce que, je crois, ne se pardonne guère,
    Vous arrachez des vers à un Anglais !

Oubliez cependant mon incartade ;—
    Mais je deviens hardi en écrivant ;
Puisque je tiens un peu du camarade,
    Souvenez-vous aussi, en oubliant.

"NAY, I'LL STAY WITH THE LAD."

(In Hutton seam, No. 3, they saw two bodies, father and son, clasped together. One of the explorers knew the man, and knew that after the explosion he had been asked by one of the men afterwards rescued to go along with him to another part of the workings, and the father replied: "Nay, I'll stay with the lad." It was the belief of the explorers that these had both died, with one or two others near, from the after-damp. They were lying peaceably, having made pillows of their jackets and clothes.—*Daily News*, September 11th, 1880.)

"Nay, I'll stay with the lad:"
 Down in the deep black seam,
Huddled together, dying and dead,
Far from the day-world overhead,
Face to face, by a sudden fate,
With a horror of Night precipitate;
Hidden away from the merciful Sun,
The death and the burial all in one,
By their fifties cut off in vain,
More than a battle counts its slain;
Huddled together, man and horse,
In the grip of the fire-damp's watchful force—
Unsung heroes of simple mould,
All unchanged from the race of old,

To the olden truths, with a martyr's cry,
Out of the depths they testify:
And never has rede been read, I deem,
Nobler than that in the deep black seam,
Of Love and Courage the message sad—
Only, "Nay, I'll stay with the lad."

"Nay, I'll stay with the lad:"
    Down in the deep black seam
They found him living, and strong, and sound,
In spite of the terror underground;
And they bade him come and live again
In the light-bright haunts of living men,
And once more look the sun in the face,
And gladden in earth's beloved embrace.
But he looked at his young boy, dead or dying,
In the midst of the shattered fragments lying—
Dying or dead—but powerless to move,
At the help of man, or the voice of Love.
And self lay dead where the child must die,
And he let deliverance pass him by;
He saw his duty set straight before
In the love that liveth for evermore,
And he put the proffered freedom behind,
With never a thought of self in mind;
And, to life or to death run the trackless stream,
He stayed with him in the deep, black seam,
And to prayer and warning one answer had,
A brave one—"Nay, I'll stay with the lad."

"Nay, I'll stay with the lad:"

    Down in the deep black seam
Once again was the story told,
Old as Honour, as Poesy old;
And the rugged miner, whose cares might be
Something unknown to you or to me,
Rather than leave his boy below,
Alone in the grip of the lurking foe,
Chose to die with him there and then,
Rather than live with his fellow-men;
Smoothed the pillow the child beneath,
Turned with him to the void of Death,
And to all mankind, in its strong self-love,
Taught the unself proclaimed above;
And whate'er his sin, and whate'er his sorrow,
Chose the night without earthly morrow—
Went to his Maker straight and free,
And pleaded his plea courageously;
For his boy he lived, for his boy he died;
And the two together, side by side,
Before the divine eternal Throne
Had nothing to plead but their love alone;
And there, perchance, from the answer prove
That the greatest wisdom of all is Love.
While wealth may prosper, denial dream,
Life's moral is told in the deep black seam;
And angels rejoice in that answer glad,
And human—"Nay, I'll stay with the lad."

A SPRIG OF HEATHER.

Dear Kate,—In Mr. Murray's Guide,
    With neat red ribbon tied together,
Between two leaves I've put aside
    Your tiny sprig of Scottish Heather.

It came to me at Berne, you know;
    I had it in a quiet corner
Of the old terrace, as the glow
    Of sunset lit the Wetterhörner.

While lower Earth outwearied slept,
    From fiery Day yet parched and torrid,
O'er the snow-pillowed giants crept
    A lazy flush from foot to forehead;

Till the grim peaks, which, cold and lone,
    Had faced the sun as if to flout it,
Now like a row of beacons shone,
    Rose-red against the grays about it.

They kindled up from horn to horn,
   And a quaint notion Fancy lent me;
Methought they crimsoned as in scorn
   Of the poor upstart you had sent me.

"The land our mighty presence fills
   Dame Nature's grandest mood discloses;
What make you, from your baby hills,
   'Mid Edelweiss and Alpine Roses?

"When men have travelled, you forget,
   The hills they've climbed, the lakes they've rowed on,
Leave little room for them to set
   Much store by Lomond or by Snowdon!

"What next?"—it was the biggest spoke;
   A mighty avalanche shook his quarters;
He cracked his glaciers at the joke,
   And shouted in a roar of waters.

I hung my head, and, half in shame,
   I looked upon your tiny token;
When out of it an answer came,
   As clearly as the first had spoken.

The little flow'ret seemed to wear
   Upon its leaf a look defiant,
And to throw back with interest there
   His scorn upon the scornful giant.

"You overgrown unsightly mass,
   (Rude challenge breeds uncivil answer),
Learn, in your innermost crevass,
   It isn't size that makes the man, sir!

"I come from lands of fern and heath,
   Which smell so sweet, and look so tender,
When the long kiss of Autumn's breath
   Has fanned them to a blush of splendour,

"That every puny half-starved flower
   Which aches upon your iron bosom,
Would give that honour for an hour
   Upon those laughing slopes to blossom,

"Or nestle in their grasses rare,
   Like jewels in a woman's tresses;
While you were born as bald, you were,
   As any head that Truefitt dresses!

"If salt is good, then how thrive you,
   Aloft there in your frigid snow-zone,
Where the best wind that ever blew
   Bears not a breath of Ocean's ozone?

"I bring you from the farther North
   A sauce your meal of ice to savour;
A single whiff of Clyde and Forth
   Gives all your air a finer flavour!

"Be more polite another day:"—
　The mountains held their tongues and whitened;
But for my life I couldn't say
　If they were most amused or frightened.

On the bold messenger I smiled—
　"True offspring of the British nation,
As for the *sauce* you bring, my child,
　You've quite enough for all creation.

"'Tis rarely that the sage, I wis,
　With any party on his oath sides,
But holds, as I do now, there is
　A good deal to be said on both sides.

"Whiche'er the better cause has shown,
　Old Scotland or the land of Tell—come,
You've one advantage all your own—
　Kate sent you, and you're very welcome!"

Berne, August, 1873.

IN TWO WORLDS.

Under the forest, of its snows unladen,
    And kissing back the nervous kiss of Spring,
I sit and dream of courtly knight and maiden,
    And old-world pomp encompassing a King.

Out of her wintry sleep the Earth is waking,
    And birds and flowers carol her *réveillée;*
O'er East and West the common promise breaking,
    Breathes the first whisper of their holiday.

Without, the mighty forms of things primæval
    Stand all untenanted of Custom's robes;
Within, my mind shapes pictures mediæval,
    With pencil fashioned forth in other globes.

The rugged miners share my board and pillow,
    And by the camp-fire sing their lawless song;
But at a bound my thought o'errides the billow,
    And breasts the strong surf by a flight as strong.

IN TWO WORLDS.

What do I here among the waving grasses,
  Which never learned to trim their graces wild?
While by my side Nature's rude army passes,
  Another world still claims me for her child.

In vain I ply the axe in pass or clearing;
  In vain I fill me with the unfettered air;
Still to my eyes are other scenes appearing,
  Still my heart hearkens the low voice of Care.

Among our ranks no woman comes to harm us,
  And sow us discord for our hands to reap;
No wiles and jars allure us or alarm us,
  Or wanton with the mighty arm of Sleep.

Yet here, for me, though heart and will are master,
  As strong as Iron and as calm as Death,
The will will waver and the heart beat faster,
  Touched by the memory of a woman's breath.

Why are ye here, rude fellows of my labour,
  Thus outlawed from the bounds of woman's reign?
Read I, beneath the swart hues of my neighbour,
  Another story of another pain?

She said she loved me; and one day she left me,
  Without a warning and without a word;
Of past and present at a blow bereft me;
  The cause unspoken, and the plea unheard.

Behind me honour, and high hopes before me—
  A life of earnest and a name of worth;
Her glamour shed the bright delusion o'er me;
  Her presence kept the promise of my birth.

Then fell the blow, and past and future shivered,
  Just at a fairy finger's heartless touch;
And from the bondage of a lie delivered,
  I laughed that I had trusted overmuch.

Laughed! and the echo of that hollow laughter
  Rings in my heart with one eternal knell;
And the slow years which rolled their burden after,
  With all the burden cannot crush the spell.

Pines of the Sierras, spread your mantles round me,
  And hide me from the past, untrodden West!
Oh that the free lands and free souls which bound me,
  Could break the fetters of my prisoned breast!

In vain, in vain! Not the dividing ocean,
  With all its storms one memory can drown;
While the vexed phantom of a lost devotion,
  Still in the tortured bosom dies not down.

Up, and to work! The western spring invites me,
  And freedom calls me forth among the free:
But no! Nor work nor freedom here delights me,
  The Eastern bondage falls again on me.

LES ENFANS DE BOHÊME.

Joyeux pays des gens joyeux,
    Les beaux esprits de ce bas monde,
Pour te donner à nos aïeux,
    Vénus sortit jadis de l'onde.
La belle reine de bonté
    Protégera tout cœur qui aime,
Et vit toujours, dans sa beauté,
    Pour les enfans de la Bohême.

Le musicien va fredonnant
    Les doux airs de son répertoire ;
Le peintre vient en exploitant
    Les belles couleurs pour sa victoire :
Le poète rêve le beau,
    Chantant en dépit de soi-même ;
Le luth—la plume—le pinceau
    Ouvrent pour nous nôtre Bohême.

La route parsémée de fleurs,
  Voici bien d'autres qui s'avancent ;
En foule viennent ces chers pêcheurs,
  Les gens qui jouent, les gens qui dansent.
Il est heureux, le Bohémien,
  Car, pour bien égayer sa serre,
Il sait trouver, sur son chemin,
  Les belles filles de la terre.

Versons le bon vin pétillant ;
  À l'avenir ne songeons guère :
Quand le sort pour nous est méchant,
  À l'avenir buvons la bière !
Nous donnons gaîment d'une main,
  Quand nous avons la bourse pleine,
Et de l'autre prenons demain
  Des bons amis qui ont la veine.

Que l'avocat ne frappe pas,
  Il trouvera la porte close,
Et n'entre pas que dans le cas
  Qu'il soit tout bonnement sans cause :
Le médecin n'en est pas vraiment,
  Qu'il tue à part sa clientèle ;
Il faut, pour y aller gaîment,
  Assez de cœur, et de cervelle.

Le dévôt maudit son voisin
  Tous les Dimanches à la messe,
Mais prêchera pour nous en vain
  Son évangile de tristesse.

Qu'il se fasse sa propre loi,
    Faisons-y guerre, et à outrance ;
Notre devise, c'est la Foi,
    La Charité, et l'Espérance.

Tout las de travail, où de vin,
    Bien doucement quand on sommeille,
Là-haut, un petit chérubin
    Sur nous exprés sans cesse veille.
Ainsi, quand au dernier moment
    La mort à notre porte sonne,
Saluons-la en souriant—
    "Viens ! je n'ai fait mal à personne."

Nous croyons à la vérité,
    La droite ligne de la vie,
De l'amour et de l'amitié
    La seule franc-maçonnerie :
Le sage ne croit à rien,
    Excepté toujours à soi-même ;
Mais le bon Dieu, qui fait tout bien,
    Chérit ses enfans de Bohême.

PEACE—AND HONOUR.*

(APRIL 19TH, 1881.)

Hushed are the sounds of party strife
   In reverence round the quiet bed,
As all the busy stream of Life
   Seems stayed beside one spirit fled:
And England sends the message on,
To West and East—A great man gone.

Strange power of Death! Once laid on him
   With gentlest touch her royal hand,
Unbidden tears the eyes bedim,
   And manliest hearts are half unmanned.
Our little discords melt and cease;
He lies in Honour—and at Peace.

Yes—honoured in the hearts of those
   Who would his living purpose cross,
By the world's law of friends and foes,
   Suspended in a country's loss;

   * Ode to the Memory of Lord Beaconsfield.

While for his peace may no man spare
His tribute to the country's prayer.

Strange power of Death! How small they seem,
   Our quarrels, grudges—all put by,
The baseless fabric of a dream,
   Beside the great reality.
We read, ere yet the clay be cold,
In deaths like this, Death's secret told.

As to her breast the generous sea
   River and rivulet draws in,
Till all the parted streams that be
   In that maternity are kin,
Even so the pale Magician charms
All minds, all wisdoms, to his arms.

He, but a few short days ago
   Held in a nation's half mistrust,
Here feared, there followed, lying low,
   Where all may trample on his dust,
Lies safe with laurels round his brow—
His party's then, his England's now.

Strong loves he conquered on his way,
   Strong as the enmities he woke,
And the loosed passions of the day
   In praise and anger round him broke:
Anger and enmity o'erthrown,
Death has for sister—Love alone.

Men called him alien, deemed him set
　　On dreams of empire not of ours,
And prone true empire to forget
　　In the long clash of jarring powers:
But England's 'scutcheon blazons still
The motto of his life—I will.

In steady purpose, steady toil,
　　He followed, and he won the prize,
Which through the senate's fierce turmoil
　　Lighted, but dazzled not his eyes;
Nor rank nor fortune smoothed the course;
He dared, and conquered, and by force.

As patient as the great should be,
　　As watchful as the purposed are,
He marked power's ebbing, flowing sea,
　　Now sparkling near, now murmuring far,
Till with strong hand he grasped the helm,
Through storm and shine to steer a realm.

And when, life's threescore years and ten
　　In the long passage overpast,
He yielded up the helm again,
　　He stood as steady to the last:
Not Cæsar's robe, when Cæsar died,
Was folded with a calmer pride.

Calmly he gave the reins of State,
   As first he held them, self-possessed;
And undismayed, as unelate,
   Turned to the love once loved the best,
And wooed, from strife of tongues apart,
The Muse of Story to his heart.

So, England's Minister, good-night!
   Nor praise nor blame can touch thee now;
Safe from the fierce and public light
   Which beat upon thy vessel's prow:
Thy place is with the great alone,
Not one's, nor other's. England's own.

SONGS AND BALLADS.

SONGS AND BALLADS.

A LIFE'S REGRET.

Turning the leaves in an idle way
Of a book I was skimming the other day,
I found a line at the end of a song,
Which keeps on haunting me all day long
With its sweet and mournful melody;
"O love, my love, had you loved but me!"
Sadder a burden could never be
Than "Love, my love, had you loved but me!"

Few words and simple; but oh, how much
The singer has told in that little touch!
How hard a story of chances lost,
Of bright hopes blighted and true love crossed,
Is heard in the whispered melody;
"O love, my love, had you loved but me!"
To many a sorrow the key may be
That "Love, my love, had you loved but me!"

I don't believe in what poets have said
Of hearts that are broken and lives that are dead;
Lives well ordered will stand to their course,
And hearts of true metal ring little the worse,
But they vibrate still to that melody;
"O love, my love, had you loved but me!"
My life is well; but what would it be,
Sweet "Love, my love, had you loved but me!"

The world rolls on and the years roll by,
Day-dreams vanish and memories die;
But it surges up with a restless pain,
That fond lost longing ever again,
Breathed in the passionate melody;
"O love, my love, had you loved but me!"
It might have been, but it cannot be!
Yet "Love, my love, had you loved but me!"

SPINNING-WHEEL SONG.

FLASH, shuttle, through the loom,
   Warp and woof blending;
Crooning, from room to room,
   Songs never ending.
What sighs my wheel to me
   In the night season?
Love still the burden be,
   Love, and unreason.

Wheel, whisper in mine ear
   Tales of true lovers;
Clear is thy note, and clear
   What it discovers.
Sing, how a maiden bright
   Cannot be lonely,
If she talk day and night,
   With her wheel only.

Flash, shuttle, whisper, wheel,
   Humming and turning!
Secrets of eld reveal,
   Scraps of love learning!
Tell me my heart is near,
   Bid me not sorrow;
Tell me he will be here
   With me to-morrow.

"RUBY WINE AND ROSY LIP."

Ruby wine and rosy lip
   I have quaffed and press'd;
Nor, while each in turn I sip,
   Know I which is best.
Tell me which is most divine,
   Ruby lip or rosy wine?

When the glass alone I hold,
   Doubtful is the bliss;
For although it cannot scold,
   Yet it cannot—kiss.
Tell me which is most divine,
   Rosy lip or ruby wine?

When I drink but woman's eyes,
   Partial is the joy;
What if there no poison lies,
   Woman may be—coy!
Tell me which is most divine,
   Ruby lip or rosy wine?

Both at once do best engage
    All my heart, in sooth,
If the wine be crowned with age,
    And the lip with youth.
Both alike are most divine,
    Rosy lip and ruby wine !

Ruby wine and rosy lip
    Give, my love, to me ;
Happy to my finger's tip
    By my trust in thee.
True love only makes divine
    Ruby lip and rosy wine.

MY SECRET.

I would not breathe my darling's name
    To sea below, or sky above;
To Nature's spies I'll ne'er proclaim
    The golden secret of my love.

In vain the stream its murmur stills,
    That secret from my breast to steal,
And lurks amid the treacherous hills,
    If echo might her name reveal.

In vain the wind mine ear deceives,
    Hushed its rude voice in whisper low,
Eavesdropping through the tell-tale leaves
    To hear her praises as I go.

The image in my soul enshrined
    Lip-service of the best would shame;
To babbling stream, or wanton wind,
    I will not breathe my darling's name.

SERENADE.

Sleep, dear, sleep! Such eyes as those, love,
   Burn so brightly all the day,
That they need the night's repose, love,
   To be trimmed, and put away.
If the vestal soul they shine in
   Always lit the flame should keep,
What should I find air for mine in?
   Sleep, dear, sleep!

Dream, dear, dream! Thy thoughts by day, love,
   Thy sweet will may rule and guide;
Slumber-winged, they fain must stray, love,
   To thy constant lover's side.
In the sleeper's fields Elysian
   They can find no better theme—
If I mingle with thy vision,
   Dream, dear, dream!

Wake, dear, wake! The sun is high, love,
   And outburns the morning star;
Only in the eyes of my love,
   Shines a glory purer far.
Brighter than the sunrise splendour,
   When the day's first blushes break,
Is the love-light true and tender;
   Wake, dear, wake!

HORATIAN ODE.

(AN IMITATION.)

HELVELLYN's height with snows is white,
   The forest branches bow and splinter;
No ripple breaks the frozen lakes,
   Then shut my door on Cold and Winter.

On my hearth-dogs pile up the logs—
   Pile high, my boy; and down your throttle
Right freely pour my "thirty-four,"
   And never spare the old man's bottle.

Leave all the rest to him who best
   Knows how to still the roar of Ocean;
To calm the wind in wildest mind,
   And hush the leaflet's lightest motion.

Fear not to stay upon the day,
   And count for gain each happy pleasure;
Be not above the game of Love,
   And featly tread the Christmas measure.

Let blood run cold when life grows old,
   Stick now to skate and tennis-racquet,
Till westward-ho the sun-wheels go,
   Then join the sports of frock and jacket.

When bright eyes smile, laugh back the while,
   And find the nook where Beauty lingers ;
Steal golden charm from rounded arm,
   Half-given, half-held, by fairy fingers.

VENETIAN BOAT-SONG.

The boatmen are calling,
  "Stalì—stalì!" *
The glory is falling
  On me—on me!
The sunlight is shaking
  The bay—the bay!
Then up and be waking;
  "Già è—già è!" *

In Venice the golden,
  To dream—to dream,
With love-stories olden,
  For theme—for theme!
The blue sky above her
  Fair sea—fair sea,
Laughs light on the lover;
  "Stalì—stalì!"

* Stalì—Già è: the cries of the Venetian gondoliers.

VENETIAN BOAT-SONG.

The waves are her highways,
   So deep—so deep !
The waters her byways,
   Asleep—asleep !
No stir in the air is,
   No sound—no sound,
Save footsteps of fairies,
   Around—around !

The clouds of the hazy
   Forenoon—forenoon,
Sleep over the lazy
   Lagoon—lagoon !
About us a glamour
   Doth move—doth move,
The sense to enamour
   Of love—of love !

The Doges are perished,
   And gone—and gone ;
The sea-bride they cherished,
   Laughs on—laughs on !
We pass through Death's portal,
   As they—as they ;
Like her, Love's immortal !
   " Già è—già è ! "

The pride of the nations,
   " Stall—stall ! "
That hath for foundations
   The sea—the sea,

Was made for a home, dear,
    For you—for you;
Then why should we roam, dear,
    We two—we two?

MARIAN MAY.

Marian May was our hamlet's pride,
    Worthy a queen to be,
For of all the maids in the country-side
    Was none so fair as she.

Her hair was like silk and her eyes like wine,
    Liquid and dark and deep;
They sparkled and danced in the broad sunshine,
    Or melted in rosy sleep.

Lovers by scores for her white hand sighed,
    Of high and of low degree,
And many came riding from far and wide,
    Her sweethearts fain to be.

The squire had plenty of golden store,
    Such as for him was meet;
And he wished no better, and asked no more,
    Than to lay it all at her feet.

But she put his gifts and his vows aside,
   Laughing, and out spake she :
"I never was born for a rich man's bride,
   So I cannot mate with thee."

The parson he came, with his face so grave,
   Gentle and sleek and prim,
And said the best way her soul to save
   Was to take and marry him.

But she only opened her eyes full wide,
   Wondering, and quoth she :
"Were there never a man in the world beside,
   You'd be far too good for me !"

The colonel he swore a right round oath :
   "Little one, be my wife !
I've scars and a pension enough for both,
   If you'll share a soldier's life."

He vowed that he would not be denied,
   Low on his bended knee ;
But she tossed her head with a pretty pride,
   Said : "I never will wed with thee !"

Robin came back from the sea one day,
   Out of the distant West;
And the child with whom he used to play,
   A woman he clasped to his breast.

She sobbed and kissed, and she laughed and cried:
 "Welcome, my love," said she;
"For woe or for weal, and whate'er betide,
 I will fare the world through with thee!"

ST. VALENTINE'S TOUR.

ST. VALENTINE jumped from his narrow bed,
    And he gave a sleepy stare;
And the good old saint he gaily said,
" It's a very long time that I've been dead,
    And I want a change of air.

" The world has been taking my name in vain
    For many a bygone day;
And though all these years in the earth I've lain
(O Lord! what a sharp rheumatic pain!)
    They chatter of me alway.

" The lad to his lassie still once a-year
    Sends pictures of me by post;
The clodhopper woos his village-dear
With a portrait grinning from ear to ear,
And the beautiful countess expects to hear,
    The soft things she likes the most.

"I've slept so long that I guess by this
   I've slept back my youth divine;
My birthday rights no more I'll miss,
But I'll wake some pretty girl up with a kiss,
   And make her *my* Valentine."

So up he rose, and he wrapped him round
   With whatever came to hand;
He saw that his flesh was firm and sound,
(For they had embalmed him in holy ground),
But he felt so cramped that the thing he found
   The hardest was how to stand.

But saints are not puzzled their legs to mend,
   And laugh at such trifles small;
He got to back him a Hebrew friend,
And he walked for a twelvemonth, straight on end,
   Round the Agricultural Hall.

As he walked he slept, as he walked he dined,
   And he walked all night and day!
While a she South African, strong of mind,
(But as ugly as you might wish to find),
   Was walking the other way.

For his every mile she her twain would do,
   And fondly on him winked she;
But though he was dead, the old saint knew
What well might be called a thing or two,
And, thought he, "Though I'm good enough for you,
   So are not you for me!"

He flies to the maidens of Spiers and Pond,
    And thinks, as their drinks he quaffs,
"Of bar-room Hebes I am not fond,
So I'll stroll up the streets of the Regent and Bond,
    And look at the photographs."

Fair Myra de Vaux from the window-pane
    Shot straight at his heart below:
He rushed to see her at Drury Lane,
But found that the shaft had sped in vain;
For, alas! her modicum of brain
    Was all in the shop-windowe.

The rose of fashion—the sweet May Fayre,
    The twin photographer's pet—
To the giddy world did the saint repair,
And she danced a cotillon with him there;
But he thought her (which made St. Valentine swear)
    The stupidest girl he met.

So he hied him away from London vast,
    And off to the country went;
To the brawny North he journeyed fast,
By a swift express on his road he passed,
(And they merrily told him that the last
    Had met with an accident).

St. Valentine sought in every place,
    And he had not wandered far,
Ere he saw two sisters of Irish race,

One dark and the other fair of face,
But like in feature, and pure in grace,
   As Irish maidens are.

A red and white rose on a common stem,
   And the saint he looked and smiled;
For he saw to the honest heart of them,
And knew that never a brighter gem
Was set in a regal diadem
   Than either pretty child.

The mark of toil the young faces wore,
   For they toiled for daily bread;
But the good saint laughed: "My search is o'er,
Your guardian I to the better shore:
My Valentines ye for evermore:"
   'Twas thus St. Valentine said.

READY, AY, READY.*

OLD England's sons are English yet,
   Old England's hearts are strong;
And still she wears her coronet
   Aflame with sword and song.
As in their pride our fathers died,
   If need be, so die we;
So wield we still, gainsay who will,
   The sceptre of the sea.
England, stand fast; let hand and heart be steady;
Be thy first word thy last: Ready, ay, ready!

We've Raleighs still for Raleigh's part,
   We've Nelsons yet unknown;
The pulses of the Lion-Heart
   Beat on through Wellington.
Hold, Britain, hold thy creed of old,
   Strong foe and steadfast friend,
And still unto thy motto true,
   Defy not, but defend.
England, stand fast; let heart and hand be steady;
Be thy first word thy last: Ready, ay, ready!

* Arranged as a song from the verses at p. 109.

Men whispered that our arm was weak,
    Men said our blood was cold,
And that our hearts no longer speak
    The clarion-note of old;
But let the spear and sword draw near
    The sleeping lion's den,
His island shore shall start once more
    To life with armèd men.
England, stand fast; let heart and hand be steady;
Be thy first word thy last: Ready, ay, ready!

SIR PAUL'S DAUGHTER.

Sir Paul had a daughter as fair and as fine
   As woman has been till now,
Her eye flashed dark as a flagon of wine,
   And white as new milk was her brow;
Her life was so rare she had never a care,
   Save to foot it in bower and in hall;
Every day lovers new like the blackberries grew
   For the daughter of old Sir Paul.

Her wit flashed as keen as a scimitar's blade,
   When carried in Moslem hand,
And love, still love, was her only trade,
   And her only whim command.
But woe, oh woe! to the captured foe,
   The wooer who came at her call,
For she pierced the heart with a deadly dart,
   Did the daughter of old Sir Paul.

Her love and her wit like the lightning shone,
   All bathed in a colour warm;
But blighted and struck where they fell anon
   With the breath of the cruel storm.
Oh, dire was the ruth of the favoured youth,
   Who for her gave soul and all!
For man or for boy it was death to toy
   With the daughter of old Sir Paul.

BRIAN BORU.

King Brian Boru was a monarch so bold,
He dressed cool in the heat, and dressed warm in the cold!
Sure never his equal on earth has been seen
For washing potatoes in kegs o' potheen;
When tired of the state and its manifold care,
Oh, he'd take his shillelagh to Donnybrook Fair,
With great condescension he'd join in the fun,
Break the heads of his subjects as if he was one,
And look such a darlin' that nobody knew
Whether he was St. Pathrick or Brian Boru.

King Brian Boru was a monarch so sly,
That he'd catch all the girls wid a wink of his eye!
He was neat, he was sweet, he was straight, he was big,
But never so great as when dancin' a jig;
He danced like a fairy that weighs twenty stone,
As the kings and the leprochauns trip it alone,
For he was a man of a wonderful kind,
And left several million descendants behind,
Till divil a one of the progeny knew
Who owned the succession of Brian Boru.

King Brian Boru had red hair to the taste,
Which in beautiful ringlets hung down to his waist !
He had eyes just as green as me favourite cat,
Which when he was angry got greener than that :
Oh, an elegant vision was Brian to see,
Wid a crown on his head and a wench on his knee !
In one hand the sceptre, in t'other the bowl :
May the angels sing rest to His Majesty's sowl,
And remark to soft music that never they knew
Such a broth of a boy as King Brian Boru !

PARODIES, ETC.

PARODIES, ETC.

THE TOWN OF NICE.

(MAY, 1874.)

The town of Nice! the town of Nice!
   Where once mosquitoes buzzed and stung,
And never gave me any peace,
   The whole year round when I was young!
      Eternal winter chills it yet,
      It's always cold, and mostly wet.

Lord Brougham sate on the rocky brow,
   Which looks on sea-girt Cannes, I wis',
But wouldn't like to sit there now,
   Unless 'twere warmer than it is;
      I went to Cannes the other day,
      But found it much too damp to stay.

The mountains look on Monaco,
   And Monaco looks on the sea;
And, playing there some hours ago,
   I meant to win enormously;

But, tho' my need of coin was bad,
I lost the little that I had.

Ye have the southern charges yet?
　　Where is the southern climate gone?
Of two such blessings, why forget
　　The cheaper and the seemlier one?
　　　　My weekly bill my wrath inspires;
　　　　Think ye I meant to pay for fires?

Why should I stay? No worse art thou,
　　My country! on thy genial shore
The local east-winds whistle now,
　　The local fogs spread more and more;
　　　　But in the sunny south, the weather
　　　　Beats all you know of put together.

I cannot eat—I cannot sleep—
　　The waves are not so blue as I;
Indeed, the waters of the deep
　　Are dirty-brown, and so's the sky:
　　　　I get dyspepsia when I dine—
　　　　Oh, dash that pint of country-wine!

MATILDA.

Shall I fret and fume and swear,
Because Matilda dyes her hair?
Or make pale my cheeks with care,
That hers so *very* rosy are?
Though her raven locks to-day
Turn as yellow as the hay,
If she be but true to me,
What care I how blonde she be!

Shall a woman's weakness move
Me such weakness to reprove?
Or her little failings known
Make me careless of my own?
Though her bills be longer than
Bill of duck or pelican,
If they be not paid by me,
What care I how long they be?

If her youth be left behind,
Shall I play the fool and mind?
She must be, the women say,
Forty-five if she's a day—

But I swear she looks no more,
At the most, than forty-four:
If she's young enough for me,
What care I how old she be?

Be she painted, fast, or old—
Be she flirt, or rake, or scold—
She has cash enough to make
Me submissive for her sake:
If she lose her money, though,
I can scorn and let her go;
If in poverty she be,
She may go to Bath for me!

ANGOT-MANIE.*

On Pyrenean mountains,
  On Margate's shrimpy sands,
Where Rhine's melodious fountains
  Roll down their German bands;
By many a rushing river,
  By Neva, Thames, and Seine,
Will none mine ears deliver
  From that eternal strain?
    "Très jolie—
      Peu polie:"
    Nothing else where'er I go!
      Oh, the bore of it!
      Please, no more of it!
    Save me from the Dame Angot!

Men will not sing the old songs;
  Their name is never heard;
For months they haven't sold songs,
  But that familiar word:

* Air: "Très jolie—peu polie!"

John, Thomas, Jane, and Mary,
  Maid, matron, man, and boy,
The minstrel from the prairie,
  The grinder from Savoy,
    Shout that ditty in
    Every city, in
  Every street and every show;
    Put a stopper u-
    Pon that opera!
  And destroy the Dame Angot!

'Frisco, whose portals golden
  Let in the golden west,
And all the cities olden,
  And all the modernest:
New York, Old York, and Cadiz,
  Coomassie, Brixton, Bray,
Ring with the market ladies'
  Refrain all night and day!
    Oh, ye deities!
    In each key it is;
  Flute, and organ, and also
    Pianoforte tune
    Up that naughty tune—
  Save us from the dame Angot!

Paris, 1874.

THE CRUISE OF THE SIX HUNDRED.

"The struggle between the labourers in Kent and the farmers who locked them out has ended in the men's departure for New Zealand. The men, it will be remembered, struck against a reduction of wages, and were then locked out till they should abandon the Union. The farmers believed that, under the pressure of the hard times, they would yield; but the younger men determined to emigrate, and introduce into the colony the cultivation of Kentish hops. The Government of New Zealand, which prefers this class of emigrants to all others, readily agreed to assist them, and on Wednesday six hundred emigrants, most of them young men, the pick of the country-side, started from Maidstone for the Antipodes... The men, according to the *Daily News*, all plead the absence of any prospect of "getting on."—*Spectator*, Feb. 1, 1879.

HALF a life, half a life,
 Half a life plundered;
As for the wage of death
 Strove the six hundred.
"Seaward," at last they said,
"Seaward our lines are laid!"
Out of the land of death
 Sailed the six hundred.

"Doubt here and dull dismay,
Yonder the dawn of day;
   England has blundered,
Ours not her mission high,
Ours not to ask her why,
Ours but to toil and die."
Out of the land of death
   Sailed the six hundred.

Home-ties in heart of them,
Home-ties in love of them,
Home-ties among them
   Severed and sundered.
"Boots not our pain to tell,
Life for a doit we sell:"
So with a long farewell
   Sailed the six hundred.

Bent every knee in prayer,
Rose every sigh in air:
"If there be plenty there,
   Long have we wondered."
Dream-bound their misery spoke,
And with a start they woke;
So the hard spell they broke—
   Broke the six hundred.

"Have we no birthright dear?
Have we but masters here?

Ever in failing fear
   Trodden and plundered.
Soldiers may die and bleed,
Slain for the devil's creed—
Ours to be free indeed!"
   Cried the six hundred.

Mourn, then, our banished sons;
Man, then, our newest guns,
Speed these our gallant ones
   From the land sundered;
Honour their hopeful heart,
Honour as they depart;
   God bless the seaward start
   Of the six hundred!

AD AQUÆ POTORES.

A MIRACLE of love divine
Changed all the water into wine :
Save me from miracles of men,
Who want to change it back again.

RHYMES FOR THE TIMES.

A WINTER'S TALE.

(SEE HORACE, BOOK I. ODE II.)

THE wretched world has had enough
Of snow and ice, and quantum suff,
    Altogether,
Of floundering over field and park,
And shivering through the light and dark,
And vain petitions to the clerk
    Of the weather.

I try to keep the cold at bay,
By storing brandy night and day
    In my cupboard;
And every pretty girl I meet
Wants to avoid me in the street,
Because her nose is red, and feet
    India-rubbered.

Man likes his skating for a bit,
But grows a little tired of it;
    Si sic semper,
Although both amiable and mild,
And very gentle from a child,
It strikes me that I may get riled
    In my temper.

Next must the times return again,
When on the wooden heads of men
    Down there fell huge
Torrents of rain—the largest out,
As Yankees say—in fact, about
The worst recorded waterspout,
    Called the Deluge?

Then did the globe, they say, become
A sort of large Aquarium,
    And their senses
The finned and feathered tribes forsook;
The thrushes swam by hook or crook,
And all the little fishes took
    All the fences.

If Father Thames should overflow
His banks for just a month or so?
    And unsparing
Of Beauty's self, upset the King-
ston Waterworks, that lovely thing,
Or the fair bridge to ruin bring
    Down at Charing!

Whom shall we call on to assuage
The Winter-God's resistless rage,
    Even while foemen
Of savage race destroy the flower
Of England's youth, and all the power
Of Evil round us seems to lower?
    Absit omen!

The good Sir Walter's moral ran,
How swift and sure from Folly man
  Into Sin goes;
Kind Heaven, the cup of Reason mix,
And save us from the conjuring tricks,
And blood-and-thunder politics
  Of the Jingoes!

February, 1879.

HÄCKEL OF JENA.

(A dinner was given last night to Professor Häckel of Jena by French *savants*. In his speech, as reported in the *Temp*, he expressed gratification at the progress of evolutionist ideas among French men of science, and remarked that professors and preachers who ridiculed man's descent from the ape unwittingly furnished the best proof of it, their pride and childish vanity being foibles which might have been bequeathed by the ape. Man, however, did not descend from any known anthropoid, but was a branch of the catarhine monkeys of the Old World. The continuity of nature was daily becoming more evident, and superstition, mysticism, and teleology would give way to reason, causality, and mechanism. Among philosophic minds, at least, the believers in final causes of the universe, immutability of species, sterility of bastards, geological cataclysms, successive creations, and the late appearance of man were dying out. The primitive life-organisms were formed chemically by spontaneous generation at the bottom of the sea, like saline crystals in water. Nohow else could the origin of life be explained. Lamarck and Darwin had struck the last blow at the doctrine of final causes, and modern morphology was irreconcilable not only with the dogma of the Creation, but with that of Providence, or the vague idealist pantheism of Hegel, Schopenhauer, and Hartmann. The transformation of living organisms under the influence of adaptation, hereditary selection, and struggle for existence could not, indeed, be mathematically demonstrated, but its existence could not be doubted any more than psychology or social science, and anomalies would soon be explained by the laws of mechanics were all the elements procurable; but the instability of the elements constituting the tissue of organised beings made biological problems very complex. The speech was much applauded.—*Times* Paris correspondence, 30th August, 1879.)

POWER to thine elbow, thou newest of sciences!
   All the old landmarks are ripe for decay;
Wars are but shadows, and so are alliances;
   Häckel of Jena's the man of the day.

HÄCKEL OF JENA.

All other ologies want an apology;
    Bread's a mistake—science offers a stone;
Nothing is true but anthropobiology:
    Häckel of J.* understands it alone.

Häckel the real evolutionist teacher is,
    Licking morphology clean into shape:
Lord, what an ape the professor or preacher is,
    Ever to doubt his descent from an ape!

"Children are you in your pride and your vanity,
    If you can laugh at a word that I say;
Naught in the world but the sheerest insanity
    Questions my apehood," quoth Häckel of J.

"Man's an anthropoid (he cannot help that, you know),
    First evoluted from Häckels of old;
He's but a branch of the catarh-ine cat, you know—
    Monkey, I mean—that's an ape with a cold!

"Daily is Nature's revealed Conte-inuity
    Pulling Causality's nose into joint;
All Teleology's but incongruity
    (What it all means is not now to the point).

"Species loses its immutability;
    Minds philosophic see naught in a cause;
Bastard Sterility's mere imbecility:
    Häckel's remarks must be taken as laws.

    * Pronounced Yay, or it wouldn't be German.

"Fast dying out are man's later appearances,
  Cataclysmitic geologies gone—
Now of Creation completed the clearance is:
  Häckel of J. you must anchor upon.

"Primitive Life-Organisms were chemical,
  'Busting' spontaneous under the sea;
Purely subaqueous, panaquademical,
  Was the original Crystal of Me!

"I'm the apostle of mighty Darwinity
  (Stands for Divinity—sounds much the same),
Apo-theistico-Panasininity
  Only can doubt whence the lot of us came.

"Down on your knees, Superstition and Flunkeydom;
  Can't you accept my plain doctrines instead?
What is so simple as primitive Monkeydom,
  Born in the sea with a cold in its head?

"Häckel's the man! but whatever the issue of
  This comprehensible practical creed,
Still I'm afraid the demonstrable tissue of
  Organised beings is complex indeed!"

Häckel was silent; they loudly applauded him,
  Highly commended his utterance tall;
All evolution respectfully lauded him—
  Then it was over. What came of it all?

WH–STL–R *v.* R–SK–N.

ON A CERTAIN *CAUSE CÉLÈBRE*, 1879.

THY Wh–stl–r's wrath, to Art the unfathomed spring
Of woes on woes, æsthetic goddess, sing !
Sing how he battled, that Columbian bold,
For outraged symphonies in black and gold;
His puny critic in full court would meet,
And laid his wrongs before the judgment-seat.
Should he, in might before his easel set,
Outwork the rapid hand of Tintoret ?
Lend with a touch to Chelsea's glowing skies
A richer hue than Titian's mightiest dyes ?
Out-Raphael Raphael in a blaze of power ?
Bid canvas live for ever in an hour ?
For Beauty's sake defy heraldic rules,
And quarter scarlet on a field of gules ?
And pour before a world tradition-sated,
In strains profuse, art unpremeditated ?
Should he do this, and more, yet knuckle down
Before a hireling scribbler's venal frown ?

"Never," quoth he, "by the mispainted sun,
In earth or heaven shall such foul wrong be done!
Forbid it, Law; forbid it, H–ddl–st–n!
What though the Forty, whom my soul abhors,
Against my genius bar their envious doors?
Time-serving slaves, unfit to black the boots
Of my large-hearted patron, great Sir C—tts!
What though T–m T–yl–r, *Punch's* showman small,
Compare my tints to paper on the wall?
What though B–rn– J–n–s, the imperceptive wretch,
Call my best 'nocturne' an unfinished sketch?
What though to R–sk–n's ignorant pretence
Better than I have bent in deference,
Whose stones of Venice, with precision hurled,
Break half the heads of the artistic world?
Though all beside submit to his abuse,—
Professor G–ldw–n Sm–th be dubbed a goose;
Fair M–rt–n—u, the famed agnostic belle,
A vulgar and a foolish infidel;
Though all his lightnings play and thunders roll
Round the white head of unrepressed Sir C–l—e,
Let me but pay the necessary fee,
Writ down a coxcomb Wh–stl–r ne'er shall be!
Art of the future, bid these minions blush;
Behold in me the W–gn–r of the brush!
Would that my fist around their orbs of view
Might paint choice symphonies in black and blue!
In Art's fair name drive we these penmen back,
Down with their discords dire in white and black;

Come forth, ye twelve, palladium of the free,
Who settle everything when ye agree,
And solve all knotty points with sure precision,
From High Art to an omnibus collision;
Come forth, and bravely do your fearless part,
Avenge in me this outrage upon Art;
And be our golden Yankee rule confest,
Whate'er is quickest done is done the best."

Spirits of Pope and Johnson, where ye sleep,
Call grinning Bathos from the vasty deep.
In melting tones the guileless P—rry spoke,
And neck and heels the Judge dragged in his joke;
The General Attorney for the Crown
Brought for the nonce his oratory down
From all the high disputes of moneyed men
To this ignoble strife 'twixt pot and pen;
The wigs wagged all around the smoke-dried court,
And of the suitors made their usual sport;
Then, when my lord would by his twelve abide,
For "much was to be said on either side,"
Amid the breathless silence of the house,
The legal mountain bore its youngest mouse,
And laid the damages to Art (if any,
In pleaders' phrase) at one-fourth of a penny.

RORKE'S DRIFT.

Nine hundred gone. Broad seas of Time
   O'er a deaf world have surged and rolled,
Since the first lowly Christmas chime
   Rang out its note of virgin gold.
Peace came two thousand years ago—
Man would not greet her. Be it so.

O fools and blind! Light from on high
   The humble soul illumines still;
But doth all purer rays deny
   To hearts full swollen in selfish will,
Though flashes, ever and anon,
Heaven's warning down. Nine hundred gone.

Fond dreamers they, whom visions nursed
   Of peaceful cures for human woes:
When the black cloud of battle burst
   Over the sad Crimean snows,
Had forty winters welcomed in
Peace, as if Christendom were kin.

Alas, how oft on England's heart
   Palled those brief years of tranquil life!
How would our wakeful passions start
   At every sound of distant strife;
Answer each cry of disaccord,
And whet for war the ready sword!

O'erpampered with each peaceful glory,
   Won, step by step, through toil and skill,
We traced our fathers' martial story,
   And would not hear the "Peace, be still!"
The angel sighed and fled from men;
And angry Battle reigned again.

Ay, reigned indeed: from shore to shore
   His devilish triumphs have been won;
And Statecraft rises, as of yore,
   To mar what better hands have done;
Till sudden as the trump of doom,
War claims of her his hecatomb.

Ye lords and rulers of the State,
   Secure in all your place and pride,
Think of the homes left desolate,
   Think of the heroes who have died;
And pause, ere mad Ambition's race
   Makes very Mercy veil her face.

What is't to us if others rave,
   When England lays her weapons down?
The island-queen, who ruled the wave,
   Wears still the iron in her crown;

Full as of old the life-blood runs
Through the great hearts of England's sons.

Not in the days of bow and spear,
   And deadly counter hand to hand—
God bless them!—knew they less of fear
   Than when, with small undaunted band,
Our Bromhead faced that savage fight
From dark to dawn, through Afric night.

Still tremble on the verge of death
   The hearts that hang on news from sea;
Still hold we back the passionate breath,
   In silent cry on bended knee;
The souls that pray, pray yet the more;
Down, ye that never prayed before!

Pray Heaven, that yet with humbled heart
   The eternal lesson we may learn,
That statesman's craft and statesman's art
   To smaller things than dust return;
And blessings new our land shall bless,
Whose strength should be in quietness.

"POSTE RESTANTE."

FROM SIR ST—FF—D N—RTHC—TE TO LORDS B—C—NSF—LD AND S—L—SB—RY.

My Lords B. and S., on a day coming round,
I shall wish myself several miles underground;
And I feel far from well as the turn we approach
So fatal to many a cabinet coach,
When politics Tory and politics Whig,
And we Ministers small and you Ministers big,
And schemes for the good of the land we adore
(To keep us in office a year or two more),
And light-hearted wars for the same noble ends,
Which *may* make our seats rather shaky, my friends,
Devices for tickling the tax-paying trout,
As Peaces with Honour, and quarrels without—
Things amusing to you, but perplexing to me,
Are brought to the Budget's hard test—£ s. d.
It's all very well to be gartered and starred,
With Orders at so many glories a yard,
While the valorous Jingoes are shouting for joy,
And dancing like fools to the tune of Dalroy,

And threatening creation till hoarse in the throat
With "Arrah! who'll tread on the tail of my coat?"
Yet here have we wasted good gallons of breath,
To harry one poor wretched savage to death,
And to find that another—the brute!—dares to stand
In arms for his country, and fight for his hand.

And just as the Clubs and the drawing-rooms, my Lords,
Keep the talk to themselves, leaving others the swords,
And bragging like Bobadils over their wine,
"D—— the tactics of Ch–lmsf–rd! just listen to mine!"
As they eat, sleep, and bluster, and sit at their ease,
While, to win you the votes of such fellows as these,
The Br–mh–ds and Ch–rds throw their lives in the van,
And half-fledged young heroes die game to a man—
Just so, for the glory and good of the Peerage,
Must we niggers of yours go to work in the steerage,
And see you beplastered with all the renown
Of the "Barons of England" who brag for the Crown,
Till, as soon as we come to the reckoning-day,
There's only myself and the D——l to pay.

My Lords B. and S., do not take it amiss,
If I hint that I've grown rather weary of this.
I'm weary of saying—so often I've said it—
That "I think that the C–mm–ns have done themselves
    credit,"
When I feel from my heart that, for better or worse,
For years they've been doing the very reverse;

"POSTE RESTANTE."

I'm weary of plying invisible soap,
Till my graceful ablutions with Gr–nv–lle's might cope!
I'm sick of denying the logic of figures;
I'm sick of O'D–nn–lls, and P–rn–lls, and B–gg–rs!
Most peaceful of men, with mankind I'm at feud,
Though H–rt–ngt–n's gentle, yet H–rc–rt is rude;
From the member for Gr–nw–ch I shrink to my shoe,
He says such unmannerly things—and so true!
And truth, as you know, is not much in your line
(Though I've a dim notion it's really in mine);
In my budget I've nothing to do but confess
That we've spent ten times more and saved ten times less
Than we ever expected to save or to spend;
And I heartily wish the whole thing at an end,
And give you a word of advice. As I guess,
The country's debauch of prolonged B. and S.,
Has given her whole Constitution a shaking;
But she's sleeping it off, and look out for the waking!
From the trail of your chariot fain would I far be
And join Cincinnatus, C–rn–rv–n, and D–rby,
Dig potatoes at P–nes, both your worships henceforth cut,
And be a good man.
     Your misled ST–FF–RD N–RTHC–TE.

1879.

THE ROYAL WEDDING.

(VIDE "THE TIMES," MARCH 14, 1879.)

I'M a reporter, bound to do
    Reporter's duty;
In language beautiful all through
    I sing of Beauty.

And he who thinks these words of mine
    Something too many,
Let him reflect—for every line
    I get a penny.

I sing of how the Red Prince took
    His pretty daughter,
To marry her to Connaught's Dook
    Across the water.

Oh, bright was Windsor's quaint old town,
    Decked out with bravery;
And blessèd Spring had ne'er a frown
    Or such-like knavery.

The sea of legs before the gate
   And round the steeple,—
In short, the marvellously great
   Amount of people,—

Instead of treading upon toes
   And dresses tearing,
Was (as a royal marriage goes),
   I thought, forbearing.

The church-bells rang, the brass bands played,
   The place was quite full,
Before the Quality had made
   The scene delightful.

They came from Paddington by scores,
   'Mid rustics ploughing,
And women huddled at the doors,
   And infants bowing.

While condescension on their part
   We quite expected,
On ours, as usual, England's heart
   Was much affected.

Whene'er we welcome Rank and Worth
   From foreign lands, it
Becomes a wonder how on earth
   That organ stands it!

* * * * *

The Berkshire Volunteers in gray
   (Loyd Lindsay, Colonel),
And the bold Rifles hold the way,
   With Captain Burnell.

To guard St. George's brilliant nave,
   Believe me, no men
Could properly themselves behave
   Except the yeomen.

Spring dresses came " like daffodils
   Before the swallow,"
On ladies' pretty forms (with bills,
   Alas! to follow).

Their beauty "took the winds of March"
   (Which in my rhymes is
A theft Shakesperean and arch:
   It is the *Times's*).

Sir Elvey played a solemn air;
   I sent a wish up;
Four Bishops came to join the pair,
   And one Archbishop.

Nine minor parsons after that
   To help them poured in;
One strange-named man among them sate,
   The Rev. Tahourdin.

But oh! how this "prolific pen"
  Of mine must falter,
When I describe the noblemen
  Before the altar!

There was the Lady Em'ly King-
  scote, like a tulip;
The Maharajah Duleep Singh,
  And Mrs. Duleep.

The gallant Teck might there be seen
  With sword and buckler,
His Mary in a dark sage green,
  And Countess Puckler.

Count Schlippenbach, the Ladies Schlie-
  fen and De Grunne,
And other names that seem to me
  A little funny.

Though from his years the child was warm,
  Prince Albert Victor
Looked, in his naval uniform,
  A perfect pictur.

The Marchioness of Salisbury
  I wondered at in
Reseda velvet draped with my-
  osotis satin.

Dark amethyst on jupes of poult
   Wore the Princesses;
And ostrich feathers seemed to moult
   From half the dresses.

Real diamonds were as thick as peas,
   And sham ones thicker—
Till overcome, your special flees
   To ask for liquor!

    *   *   *   *   *

The show is o'er: by twos and twos
   I see them fleeting off,
Lord Beaconsfield, the *Daily News*,
   And Major Vietinghoff.

The happy couple lead the way,
   For life embarking;
Then Captain Egerton and La-
   dy Adela—Larking.

Louisa Margaret! to thee
   Be grief a stranger,
And may thy husband never be
   A Connaught Ranger.

If in the blush of mutual hopes,
   And fond devotion,
You're honeymooning on the slopes,
   I've not a notion.

But this I feel, that for your true
   And honest passion,
All sober folks wish well to you
   In manly fashion.

While, for your chroniclers, I know,
   Regnante V.R.,
From east to west 'twere hard to show
   Such men as we are!

BEN-BASTES FURIOSO.

I am the Peerless Premier,
    'Tis mine to speak, and yours to hear.
Intelligent England! now the time has come,
    As all must own
    And see,
When you must rally round Me and the Throne—
    Particularly Me:
Or else the random rage of ruthless Rome,
The fickle falsehood of fair-fawning France,
Bismarckian braggadocio from Berlin,
The mystic Muscovite's most monstrous maw,
Home-rulers hoarsely howling hideous hum—
    Bug,
    Where smug
They batten on their melancholy isle;
    And worse (I smile
At thought of their exuberant verbosity,
    Intoxicated with jocosity,
    And animosity),
The lagging Liberal leaders, limp and little
("Loyal" begins with *l*, and that's a pity),
William, the would-be-witty,
And he, that wilier William, the chief curse
Of the utterly unbounded Universe,
    Will whittle

The British Constitution, Queen, and Me
(Throwing in N–rthc–te, Cr–ss, and S–l–sb–ry),
Away at once; and, England, you will find
    Nothing behind
    Except a policy of Decomposition,
    Purposing Partition,
    Precipitation of Disintegration,
    And Holocaust of Humbug. (*Aside.*) What am I at?
I don't mean that.

    England! the Man is here!
    For Benjamin and Beer!
    England, go in and win!
    For Beer and Benjamin,
    Whose mess is five times more
    Than Minister's was before,
    (As erst in Hebrew writ
    A youth foreshadowed it);
Vote down, 'mid Jingo, Jug, and Jollity,
The imps of irresponsible frivolity;
Vote up the Anti-Art-of-Agitation,
The Angelic Author of Augurisation,
Apotheosis of Alliteration,
At once the A, and O, and B
    (That's Me);
    The Man of Mystery,
    The Heart of History,
    The Scourge of Savages
    (Which rhymes to "ravages"),

>   The Light of L–tt–n,
>   (What rhyme to hit on?)
>   And here I pause,
>   Because,
> As I proceed, I find my power grows small
> To rhyme or scan at all.
>
> What's that to Me, whose clarion Caucasian
> Has by Tall Truth saved England from invasion,
> Remade the world, and given new rope
>   To exhausted Europe?
> (I ever mix my metaphors, for choice;
> Mixtures are potent on the popular voice.)
> Yet, Tancred, stay; thine earnest eloquence curb;
> For here I do perceive my sentences,
>   By dangerous degrees,
>   Of sense and syntax all bereft:
>   I know not where I left
>   My verb.
> So, England, think! I am the Monarch of Men!
> And I am ready to come in again:
> No matter about the others, for you see
>   The State—that's Me.
>   Reject me? Oh, you won't!
>
>   Now, don't!
> For if you do—oh, perdurable shame
> To thy brand-new Imperial name!—
> You may be called upon, some early day,
>   Once more to pay
>   Your way!
>
> *March*, 1880.

THE HEART OF MIDLOTHIAN.

(W. E. GL–DST–NE.—MARCH, 1880.)

Clearer than the note of trumpet, pealing to the Islands forth,
Borne upon the ringing echoes of the strong and steadfast North—
To the folly of the foolish, to the blindness of the blind,
Crushing down with voice of manhood half the childhood of Mankind,
Thou hast spoken well and bravely, though the threescore years and ten,
Which of old the royal Psalmist shadowed to the strength of men,
Have, in true God-fearing courage, o'er thy life of purpose sped,
And have left their mark, as ever, on the loved and honoured head.
If thy strength be toil and sorrow, Prince to us, we turn to thee:
Feed our strength from out thy weakness—joy for us such sorrow be!

Chief of all we hold the dearest—looking ever as of yore
To the Pole-star set to guide us in the Heaven for evermore—
Fearless of the cry of faction, though the people's puzzled will
For a time be swayed against thee, steady for the people still—
Careless of a Court's disfavour, smiling such disfavour down,
Jealous more than fawning courtiers for the honour of the Crown—
Speed thee in the course thou steerest, speed thee He thou serv'st so well;
Men may think the servant stumbles; such a servant never fell.
Whence, but from a source eternal—whence, but from a power divine,
Ever yet has time-worn statesman gathered such a strength as thine?
Rivals yet in word may spurn thee—ay, and to thy latest hour
Fate may still in seeming grace them with the symbolry of Power:
And, if so the will has willed it, standing as He willed to stand,
With the universal framework in the hollow of His hand,
Thou the first to feel and own it, thou the first to bend and bow;
Thou hast done thy best and manliest, not a rood hast yielded thou.

Therefore, when old Time surrenders his imperial diadem,
And upon the grave of Story writes its final requiem;
When the glistering sands of Statecraft perish in the whelming tide,
Temples reared to Wrong and Falsehood fall to ruin side by side;
When the idol Self is tumbled from that pedestal of hers,
Laughingstock of men and angels, with her startled worshippers;
When the mists of Doubt are scattered in the sudden Sun of Truth,
And the wearied face of Honour puts on an immortal youth;
Where the laurel waits the patient, where the prize is for the sure,
Where the conscious Rest eternal waits the vexed ones who endure,
Thou at least—or Faiths are fables, and the truth of truths a lie—
Hast thy welcome waiting for thee where the welcomes shall not die.

VÆ VICTIS.

In showers of gold and tinsel and enamel,
    The storms of Fate knocked down our Gessler's hat;
But, gorged and fat with Ministerial camel,
    Say, shall we swallow the Northampton gnat?
Shall we, who did all sorts of things at Berlin
    (Though what precisely has been never known),
Yet failed by that to keep our mighty Earl in,
    Not rally still around the Church and Throne?

O noble army of D–sr—li's martyrs,
    Can we not spare our land this crowning shame?
Amid a galaxy of stars and garters
    Ye have, alas! departed as ye came;
But, though ye raised, in unison harmonic,
    The swelling chorus of "your noble selves,"
And gave us powder for a wholesome tonic,
    Which puling Peace had wasted on the shelves;
And though ye freely gave the blood of others,
    And store of others' treasure freely spent,
What good were Benjamin and all his brothers,
    If Mr. Br–dl—gh sits in Parliament?

VÆ VICTIS.

Was it for this we saw the star of Honour
   Shine ever brighter o'er our cherished land,
While every Christian blessing fell upon her,
   As if at last Millennium were at hand?
Was it for this, that truthfulness unswerving
   Marked every word that dropped from S–l–sb–ry's tongue?
For this, that B––c–nsfi–ld's unselfish serving
   Has set a pattern to the Tory young?

Was it for this we sate, enthralled and moulded
   By fiery N–rthc–te's adamantine will?
Or listened, with closed eyes and arms enfolded,
   To Cr–ss's silvery speech, seductive still?
Was it for this, that one should sit beside us,
   To take an oath or leave it nothing loath?
Think of the difference, whate'er divide us,
   Between an affirmation and an oath!

O gentle Cr–nbr––k, and majestic M–nn–rs!
   O C––rns, contemptuous of a legal plea!
Clear was our conscience 'neath your stainless banners,
   Ye patterns of an olden chivalry.
Not in our rule could Peace dishonour Glory—
   We would not back the weak against the strong;
What minister, that boasts the name of Tory,
   Ever apologised when he was wrong?
Oh, abject shame! O sole surviving scion
   Yet left of H–m–lt–n's historic stock,
Well might'st thou wag thy tail, deserted lion,
   And blush all over at so rude a shock!

"Fais ce que je veux, advienne que pourra;" was
    The motto of our chief through thick and thin,
And blind obedience to the guiding star was
    Our answering principle, to keep him in.
We are not clever, and full well he knew it,
    Who led us blithely by the willing nose;
Oh, mystic mantle! if aside he threw it,
    Would all his stout Elishas come to blows?

We gave him all, and chuckled when he sold us,
    And broke the Ten Commandments at his nod;
We would have broken twenty, if he told us,
    In adoration of our Jingo-God.
For him we left the old and honest highways,
    With secret bargains smuggled in the dark,
And wildering strayed in Statecraft's stifled byways,
    Till thorns and thistles hid Light's smouldering spark.

For him we warred, with the light heart of Madness,
    And risked the Nemesis of Mercy lost;
Played with Invasion's bitter wanton sadness,
    And never counted, but concealed, the cost.
For him we talked of War, and played at Murder,
    And offered hecatombs of helpless lives;
And rough-rode England till the rowel spurred her
    Into the need that is, when Danger drives.

The cry of Conscience gave the note of warning,
    The arm of Honour sped the angry bolt;
And Truth and Freedom woke from night to morning,
    Into one strong victorious revolt.

Then hip and thigh our startled host was smitten,
   Then all our glories crumbled to a fall;
And thus we found our pedigree was written—
   " By Jingo out of Office "—after all !

June 12, 1880.

THE STORM.*

(JANUARY, 1881.)

DAME NATURE, perusing the newspaper page,
Jumped out of her bed in a deuce of a rage;
And swore by all Saints to the Calendar known,
She would prove on the spot she'd a will of her own.
"I have waited and waited," quoth she, "by the Mass,
In the hope things might come to a likelier pass;
When sham 'Peace and Honour' were kicked out o' door,
I swore to give England a chance or two more.
In return for that kicking, I gave her a year
To the heart of the Briton I thought might be dear;
With a warm sun above him, a kind earth below,
And seasons as true as the ocean at flow—
When crops might all flourish, and harvest increase,
And Trade lift her head for a worthier peace;
When Zulus and Afghans might rest on their oars,
And B–rtle be fêted on civilised shores;
I drank power to his elbow, though under the sun
B–rtle's elbow had wrought all the harm to be done—

* Such as of late o'er pale Britannia passed.—ADDISON.

THE STORM.

Believing, at least, the small reason of men
Would prevent him from shaking that elbow again.
I bowed out my D–zzy, nor grudged him the while
Of my sister, Dame Fortune, the kindliest smile,
(For though Truth in the end should compel us to flee him
We both of us know a big man when we see him):
I bowed in my Gl–dst–n–, right worthy to share
Once more in the 'will of the popular air;'*
And to warm-hearted Erin I hoped to impart,
To her brains, just a glow from the warmth of her heart.

O frustra! nequidquam! in vain I rehearse
My sinking of heart in my querulous verse,
Be the end of the play in a sock or a buskin,
'Twill drive us at last to the moral of R–sk–n—
That rival ratcatchers as worthily strive
For rule, as the best politicians alive!
For, for good or for ill be their purpose and aim,
The rats that they hunt will be always the same.
Obstructives obstruct who obstructed before,
And Parliament meets to be merely a bore;
By Tories created, by Tories deplored,
In the Queen's House of Commons mere Brass is the lord;
Sleek N–rthc–t– calls angels and saints to his aid,
And like Frankenstein shrinks from the monster he made,
And while his poor hands he in humbleness rubs,
The Tory bear-leader is led by his cubs;

* Arbitrio popularis auræ.

St. Stephen's still echoes the infantine Ch–rch–ll
(Whose pedagogues, surely, used ruler and birch ill,
When they fostered the pea in its juvenile pod,
And ruined the child by avoiding the rod).
While S–l–sbr–y utters his figments serene,
Still Anarchy stalks o'er the desolate scene ;
Nor Br–ght, nor M–nd–lla, nor D–lke, has pretence
To infuse in the mixture one tittle of sense.

The O'Shine, the O'Paque, the O'Brian Boru,
Give the best of bad brains their own land to undo ;
O'Tongs and MacHammer keep pounding away,
The first half the night, and the second all day,
With never a glimmer of wit to the fore,
All powerless to speak, and all-powerful to bore—
Till Ireland's dead Currans indignant disclaim
The darkness of dulness now linked with her name.

Historic McC–rthy, on history nursed,
Tries to make of his 'own times' the weakest and worst ;
P–rn–ll plays the stalest of demagogue play,
To be called 'King P–rn–ll' talks his country away ;
And while England, awake to the wrongs of the past,
The mantle of Love over Erin would cast,
Bad landlords would banish, good tenants would bless,
And kiss a loved sister with sister's caress,
These self-seeking weaklings, of Pigmydom born,
Make Ireland a desert, and England a scorn.

If there's not in the wide world a valley so sweet
As that in whose bosom the bright waters meet,

THE STORM.

Oh! sad was that valley when luckless she fell
To thee and to thine, cattle-maiming P–rn–ll!

What differs the past from the present, I pray?
Wherein, please, is yesterday worse than to-day?
The floor of your Commons is held by the men
Who held it before, and now hold it again;
Dishonour the master, and honour trod down,
And N–rthc–t– submissive to S–l–sb–ry's frown,
The country, o'erweary, o'erpatient, o'erworn,
Uprising in murmurs of infinite scorn,
And asking wherein, to those that have eyes,
Between 'Whig' and 'Tory' the difference lies.
I am weary of all of you—weary and sad—
Where weak beyond weak seems the best to be had;
Since for Right and for Reason no strength ye have got,
By the Lord of Creation, I'll 'Boycott' the lot!"

Dame Nature arose, in her infinite strength,
In the depths of her spirit outwearied at length;
The East wind and North wind she summoned to throw
Over Earth, Sea, and Heaven her masterful snow:
She "boycotted" London from Kew to Mile End,
Bade Thames to the tempest his armoury lend,
She locked up two Judges forlorn and alone,
And forced on the House a *clôture* of her own:
She blocked the steel rails man-invented to prove
That man was the master of force from above;
She laughed at his mission, she mocked at his word,
And through the loud storm-drift her warning was heard:

"Ay! speak from the West, and foretell to a day
When the storm-cloud shall break, and the lightning shall
    play;
Foretelling is folly, and knowledge for fools,
For the wisest of men keep the oldest of rules:
Ye fret me, ye stir me, ye move me to mirth,
At your Lownesses crawling 'twixt Heaven and Earth.
My tide it shall gather, my storm it shall burst,
In their own thoughts alone, sirs, your last shall be first:
In an hour of the tempest, a frown of the cloud,
I stoop to the humble, I threaten the proud."

BOOK C, ODE I.

It was t'other day that I chanced to range
Somewhere about the old Exchange,
As worthy old Horace erewhile would stray
By accident down the Sacred Way,
For no worse reason than this—because,
With nothing to do, it his custom was.
Bored with Earnest, and dazed with Light,
I was doing nothing with all my might,
With scarcely a thought in my idle head
But the outside number of hours in bed
Which a man brought up on Solomon's lore
Can spend at a stretch—ten hours, or more—
Blessing, with all my power to bless,
The gift of a random idleness;
Not Hyde Park idleness, blank and bland—
Time-killed, not time-killing, hand o'er hand,
And the listless misery Boredom brings
To the Crutch-and-Toothpick crown of things—
But the happy rest of a grateful brain,
Whose pulse means pleasure, whose rack means pain,

In the calm conclusion that here for us
The truth is the truth of Democritus,
And in mazes of error he least must err
Who strays with the laughing philosopher:
By the old Exchange—but, oh, what a pen this is,
Whose beginning is such a long parenthesis!

O'er the old Exchange, when you go there next,
You may see up-written an old-world text,
With a claim of property quite outworn,
And a very proper source of scorn
To all who, nursed on the prose of Time,
Hold it food but fit for the trifler's rhyme.
The great first Alpha's day has fled,
And our alphabet starts with the new "Y Z;"
(Good Lord! that a punster should dare to come
Where angels, small blame to them, are dumb!)
For Man is so great, if you rightly take him,
That none but himself ever dared to make him.
How else shall he prove, *when* his proofs prevail,
That his pointed moral adorned a tail?
When Tories, compact of faith and bad law,
Use God as a boot for kicking Br–dl—gh,
What text more meet for the sage's scoff,
Than "The Earth is the Lord's, and the fulness thereof"?

Oh sure, thought I, as I pondered o'er
The wondrous wisdom of D–n—ghm–re
(And no feeling just now the land has on her more
Than merely this—Who the deuce *is* D–n—ghm–re?),

And searched in vain in my catechism
For the duties we owe to landlordism,
Whose private decalogue's chief defence is
The "fabulæ Salisburienses"—
Oh sure, thought I, we shall learn, ere long,
That here's another good stop gone wrong,
And know, for our proper admonition,
From S–l–sb–ry's own "revised edition,"
That a newer reading must be preferred;
An apostrophe slipped in that same fifth word,
And never a soul need be perplexed
To read the sense of the poor old text:
To our Gessler's pole our caps we doff,
For "The Earth is the *Lords'*, and the fulness thereof."

TRANSLATIONS.

TRANSLATIONS.

REMEMBRANCE.

FROM THE FRENCH OF ALFRED DE MUSSET.

When back I ventured to this sacred spot,
    I thought to suffer, while I hoped to weep;
Thou dearest of all graves, yet minded not,
    Where only memories sleep.

What feared ye then, friends, of this solitude?
    Why sought ye thus to take me by the hand,
Just when old habit and old charm renewed
    Led me to where I stand?

I know them in their bloom, the hills and heath—
    The silver footfalls on the silent ground—
The quiet walks, sweetened by lovers' breath
    Where her arm clasped me round:

I know the fir-trees in their sombre green ;
 My giant-friends, that murmuring along
The careless byways of the deep ravine,
 Once lulled me with their song :

The copses, where my whole youth as I pass
 Wakes like a flight of birds to melody :—
Sweet scenes, fair desert where my mistress was,
 Have ye not looked for me ?

Oh, let them flow ; I love them as they rise
 From my yet bleeding heart, the welcome tears ;
Seek not to dry them ; leave upon mine eyes
 This veil of the dead years !

Yet will I with no vain lament alarm
 These echoing woods that in my joys had part ;
Proud is the forest in its tranquil charm
 And proud, too, is my heart.

In idle moan let others waste the hours,
 Who kneel and pray beside some loved one's bier ;
All in this place breathes life ; the churchyard flowers
 Grow not nor blossom here.

Athwart the leafy shade, bright moon, I see thee ;
 Thy face is clouded yet, fair queen of night ;
But from the dark horizon thou dost free thee,
 Widening into light.

REMEMBRANCE.

As 'neath thy rays, from earth yet moist with rain,
    The perfumes of the day together roll,
So pure and calm springs my old love again
    From out my softened soul.

The troubles of my life are past and gone ;
    And age and youth in fancy reconciled :
This friendly valley I but look upon,
    And am once more a child.

O mighty Time ! O light years lightly fled !
    Ye bear away all tears and griefs of ours ;
But ye are pitiful, and never tread
    Upon our faded flowers.

All blessings wait upon your healing wing;
    I had not thought that wound like mine could wear
So keen an edge, and that the suffering
    Could be so sweet to bear.

Hence, all ye idle names for frivolous woes,
    And formal sorrow's customary pall,
Paraded over bygone loves by those
    Who never loved at all.

Dante, why saidst thou that no grief is worse
    Than to remember happiness in woe ?
What spite dictated thee that bitter verse,
    Insulting misery so ?

Is it less true that there is light on high—
    Forget we day—soon as night's wings are spread?
Is't thou, great soul, sorrowing immortally,
    Is't thou who thus hast said?

Nay, by yon torch whose splendour lighteth me,
    Ne'er did thy heart such blasphemy profess;
A happy memory on earth may be
    More real than happiness.

THE FIFTH OF MAY.*

FROM THE ITALIAN OF MANZONI.

I.

He was. As still as lay
The cold unconscious clay,
When the last sigh of life had fled,
Of that great soul distenanted,
So, at the startling tale,
The breathless world grows pale;
In silence stands to ponder o'er
The fatal page closed evermore,
Nor knows if it may be
That mortal such as he
Shall with red footfall stain
The insulted dust again.

* The anniversary of the death of the First Napoleon.

II.

In splendour, on his throne
I saw him, and passed on:
While Fortune, blending smile and frown,
O'erthrew and raised and hurled him down,
    Amid the clamorous throng
    I scorned to wake my song:
Unskilled to flatter or to sting,
Incense nor outrage would I bring;
    But when the lustre splendid
    In sudden darkness ended,
    Rose with a start to pay
    The tribute of my lay.

III.

    From Alp to Pyramid,
    From Moscow to Madrid,
His ready lightnings flashed and shone,
Vaunt-couriers of the thunderstone,
    And lit that sea and this,
    Scylla and Tanais—
Was this true glory? Answer ye
That are not, but that are to be;
    We at Thy footstool bow,
    Maker and Lord, for Thou
    Hast of Thy master-hand
    Never such marvel planned.

IV.

The stormy joys that fret
The soul on greatness set,
The yearning of the restless heart,
That burns to play the imperial part,
And wins a guerdon higher
Than Madness durst desire—
All this was his; 'twas his to claim
For peril's meed yet greater fame;
Flying, and conquering;
An exile, and a king;
Twice in the dust o'erthrown,
Twice on the altar-stone.

V.

He uttered but his name,
And at his bidding came
Two warring centuries to wait
Upon his pleasure as their fate;
He set, with steadfast mien,
His judgment-seat between;
Then like a vision passed, and wore
His life out on that narrow shore,
A mark for boundless spite,
And pity infinite,
For hate as deep as Hell,
And love invincible.

VI.

As whelm the waters dread
　　The shipwrecked swimmer's head,
While ever and anon his eye
Strains upward in his agony,
　　And sweeps the pitiless main
　　For distant shores in vain—
So slowly o'er that sinking soul
Did the full flood of memories roll;
　　Oft on the eternal pages,
　　Wherein to after ages
　　He strove his tale to tell,
　　The listless fingers fell.

VII.

Oft, as the lazy day
Died silently away,
Earthward the flashing eye subdued,
And with enfolded arms he stood,
　　While o'er his thought was cast
　　The shadow of the past;
Again the tented squadrons sprang
To arms, again the ramparts rang;
　　Surged the bright ranks again,
　　And wave of mounted men,
　　And to the word of flame
　　The instant answer came.

VIII.

Well might the spirit die
In such an agony;
But, strong to succour, from above
Came down a messenger of love,
Raised him from his despair
To breathe a purer air,
And set his feet upon the way
Where Hope's fair flowerets bloom for aye,
To those eternal plains,
Rich in unmeasured gains,
Where man's brief glories fade
In silence and in shade.

XI.

O fair and healing Faith!
Triumphant over Death,
Write thou among thy victories,
That loftier majesty than his
Ne'er bent in humbled pride
To Christ the crucified:
Let not the light or mocking word
Be near the wearied ashes heard;
The Lord of weal and woe,
Who raises and lays low,
A living glory shed
Around the desolate bed.

SONG OF THE NIGHT.

FROM THE ITALIAN OF GIACOMO LEOPARDI.*

Thou silent orb of Night,
  What dost thou in the Heaven?
  Thou risest up at even,
And o'er the desert throw'st thy light,
    To sink at day;
    Answer, and say,
Hast thou not yet too weary found
The gray hills' everlasting round?
    Irks it thee not for aye

---

* Giacomo Leopardi (born 1798, died 1837) was one of the first of the Italian poets of the last half-century. A constant victim to disease and suffering, he was incapable of sustained composition on a large scale, and his principal poems are "Canti" and "Canzoni." Of these, perhaps the best known is the "Canto Notturno," of which the present free translation (for neither the metre nor the words of the original admit of an exact rendering) is submitted to the reader.

The author is supposed to be speaking in the person of a shepherd belonging to one of the wandering tribes who pasture their flocks on the wide plains of Central Asia.

SONG OF THE NIGHT.

On the broad plain's monotony to gaze?
How like to thine pass the poor shepherd's days!
   He rises with the sun,
     Drives to the field his flocks, and sees
     Fountains, and flocks, and trees—;
   Then, his task done,
   Lies wearily down at eventide,
   And asks for naught beside!
     Oh, tell me, of what use may be
     His life to him, or thine to thee?
     Oh, tell me, whither tend,
     And to what end
These our brief pilgrimages,
Or thine eternal course throughout the changeless ages?

   A weak old man, with whitened hair,
   Half-clad, with bleeding feet and bare,
   Bowed down beneath a heavy load,
   Unresting on his onward road—
   Where their grim watch the mountains keep,
   Where quicksands lurk, and forests sleep—
   Through burning sun and blinding rain,
   Through wind and storm and hurricane,
   Through summer heats and winter snows,
   Upon his breathless course he goes,
   O'er broken rock, by torrent lone,
   Stumbles—falls—rises—hurries on—
   He may not pause, he must not rest,
   Though wounded, bloody, sore oppressed,

Till, all his pains and perils past,
What is the goal he finds at last?—
A vast abyss, a headlong fall,
And mere oblivion covers all.
    Such, virgin moon, the span
    And life of man.

With pain he draws his earliest breath,
And o'er the cradle broods the shadow of Death:
    Even from his natal morn
        Sorrow and suffering lie first before him;
    And to console him that he e'er was born,
        Is their first care, that bore him.
        Then ever, as he grows,
In deed and word they soothe him, and sustain
His trembling footsteps on the path of pain,
        And for Life's woes
        Bid him take heart, and be
Strong for the weary road of sad Humanity.
    This is the choicest boon they give,
    The parents to the child: but wherefore then
    Must they thus force us to the light, and save
        And rear us to be men,
But to console us for the gift they gave?
    If life is wretched, wherefore must we live?
        Such, spotless moon, are we
        Of this mortality;
But thou, that art not mortal, but divine,
Turnest a deaf ear to these words of mine.

And yet perchance, lone pilgrim of the night,
Keeping thy thoughtful watch for evermore,
Thou read'st the riddle of the world aright,
Why men must bear so much, and grieve so sore:
Thou knowest what Death is, that from the face
Blots all the colours with one terrible hue;
And to what end thus, in a moment's space,
We perish out of all we loved and knew:
Nature for thee has a sure note of warning,
Which to thy vision all her purpose clears—;
The meaning of the Evening and the Morning,
And of the silent, infinite march of years;
Thou knowest why Spring's kisses wake the hills,
And why the Summer burns, and why the Winter chills.

It must be that thou knowest all these things,
Though hidden from the simple shepherd's eyes;
Or so I dream, in vague imaginings
Watching thy silver silence in the skies,
Where on their broad bounds close Heaven's distant bars;
And while my dull flocks slowly follow me,
I look upon the Night aflame with stars,
And ask within me, what all this may be!
What means this infinite vault, and this profound
And infinite serenity on high,
And the great solitude that girds us round?
Oh, what are all these things, and what am I?

'Tis thus I wonder with myself—in vain :
Creation's uses are all dark to me ;
The royal Heaven's immeasurable plain,
And the unnumbered stars' bright company ;
And all the ceaseless toil, and mad endeavour,
Of things in Heaven and things upon the Earth,
Which turn and turn, for ever and for ever,
But to return where they had first their birth— :*
The fruit and purpose of all these I miss,
Which, fair immortal, thou interpretest ;
But all I know and all I feel is this,
That from the restless round of their unrest,
And even from me, frail waif, others may borrow
Some use or some content—to me my life is sorrow.

    Happy, my flocks, are ye,
    That know not your own misery !
    How do I envy you your lot !
        Nor only so,
        Because ye sorrow not,
    And that all terror, pain, distress,
    Are in a moment's time forgot,
    But that ye never chanced to know
        Life's utter weariness.

---

  * Perhaps the unconscious tribute of the poet to the great Ποιητής of all. "The spirit shall return to the God who gave it." The translator is happy to be able to disclaim for his own part, while feeling the beauty of the Italian poem, all sympathy with the despair, born of suffering, which pervades it.—H. C. M.

SONG OF THE NIGHT.

Lapped in the soft shade, on the growing grasses,
Ye cheat the time in indolent repose;
But, though for me as peacefully it passes,
      No peace my spirit knows:
  Verdure and shade invite in vain,
Some strange spur goads me with an aching pain;
    The more I rest, the more upon me grows
      This dull unrest of brain.
  Yet have I naught to ask, naught to lament;
  As idle as your joy my discontent—
  But, though I cannot measure
  Whence or how great your pleasure,
      Happy, my flocks, are ye!
      Would ye could find a voice,
      To tell why ye rejoice,
And that which gladdens you so wearies me!

O gentle flock! O silver moon! had I
      Wings o'er the clouds to fly,
      And one by one the stars to number,
      Or like the thunder leap
      Headlong from steep to steep,
Then might my soul rouse from its dreary slumber
To happier waking; or too well it may be
  That mine is but the common doom of Earth;
  And whatsoe'er their lot, where'er their way be,
Fatal to all things born must be their day of birth.

FORTUNIO'S SONG.

(FROM THE FRENCH OF ALFRED DE MUSSET.)

Truce to your guesses, friends, I pray,
    They miss their aim;
I wouldn't for the world betray
    My lady's name.

Toast, if you will, her pretty face
    And golden hair;
For she is of the xanthous race—
    Ripe grain less fair.

Her wayward fancy's lightest mood
    Is law to me;
I'd give my life to do her good,
    Right willingly.

The pangs of passion unconfessed
    I must endure;
I feel their torture in my breast,
    Ay, past all cure.

But I have set my love too high
    To tell its aim;
And for my darling I can die
    Nor breathe her name.

THE LEGEND OF THE SWORD-HILT.

(FROM THE SPANISH OF ECHEGARRAY.)

LISTEN to the legend olden
Of Alvaro de Moncada,
Who in Seville wooed and wedded
Beatrix, the pearl of girlhood,
In an hour for him ill-fated—
In an hour for her unhappy.
Deep their love was—deep and burning!
And whene'er they rode together,
Would the passers-by look on them
As upon a mortal marvel.
But things mortal have an ending—
And the ending may be fearful!
Deep is ocean—who can sound it?
You may see it clear and tranquil,
Crystal to the eye and seeming;
But beneath that sheet of crystal
Lie the mud and treacherous quicksand.

But I wander from my story:
Turn we to our noble lady
Beatrix, the fair and stately;
Fair and radiant as a glory!
From the proud King of Granada
Came a gallant Moorish noble:
As Granada's legate came he;
Fair of face as some archangel,
Came he to Moncada's palace.
Beatrix he loved and courted;
But men said he found her cruel;
Said so—when, his mission ended,
Back returned, his suit rejected,
That bold pagan to Granada.
But the ways of Fate are crooked,
Strange and wonderful her ways are!
Why, within her costly closet,
Did the lady hide and treasure
Just a little letter, written
By the gallant Moorish noble?
'Twas, they say, a farewell letter,
Showing how that Christian lady
Had refused to his devotion
The proud heart and love he sued for.
Ne'ertheless, 'tis truly proven
That sometimes, beneath an arbour,
In her sweet and flowery garden—
Sometimes in her fragrant chamber
Languidly at ease reclining—

Oftener, when the silver moonlight
In Guadálquivîr was mirrored,
On that luckless paper reading,
Would the lady con and question
Its eternal lamentations!
It was night—the moon was shining
Like a silver throne above her;
And she read that paper over,
And then, reading, wept upon it!
Suddenly a hand behind her
Seized upon the paper—sudden
Was the cry the lady uttered;
Sharp and guilty, for before her,
Face to face, her lord was standing.—
Don Alvaro de Moncada.

What between those two then happened,
Was not known—no echo ever
Reached the outer world about them:
But—the lady died. 'Twas over.
In Toledo, Don Alvaro
Chose the blade his heirs must carry,
And within, the hilt is hollow;
And a chattering page reported
That he saw Moncada place there,
In the hilt, a blood-stained paper.
To the wars Alvaro hurried;
And men tell how in a battle
In the fair land of Granada,

He was seen, unlaced his helm,
And his mail-shirt rent and broken,
Hand to hand in single combat
With a noble Moor engaging.
Brave the Moor was; but he hurled him
To the earth, and fixing on him
Steady eye and glance of lightning,
Right across his bleeding forehead,
Where to death the Moor lay bleeding,
With his falchion's hilt he struck him.

So they tell—and tell us further,
That from that day ever onward
Every chieftain of Moncada,
Should extremity confront him,
In the hollow of his sword-hilt
Bears the signet of his honour.

SACRED VERSE.

SACRED VERSE.

PALINGENESIS.

God spake in a voice of thunder,
   Of old from Sinai's hill;
And the mystic words of wonder
   Thrill the believer still;
He sees in the vault above him,
   With the eye of Faith alone,
Gemmed round by the souls that love Him,
   The great Creator's throne.

He sees—in the day of danger—
   The column of cloud that led
From the land of the alien stranger,
   His Israel whom he fed;
And knows—though his footsteps wander
   Astray in a twilight land—
That his home is building yonder,
   By the one unerring Hand.

He sees—in the night of peril—
    The pillar of fire that shone
From the halls of pearl and beryl,
    To light God's children on ;
And feels, that straight from Heaven,
    When the eye of sense grows dim,
Shall a grander sight be given
    To all who trust in Him.

On the page of the mighty ocean
    He reads the Mightier still,
Who curbs its restless motion
    By the law of His royal will :
And while in its course diurnal
    It murmurs, or sings, or raves,
He lists to the voice Eternal,
    In the language of the waves.

He marks in the plants around him
    The throbs of a life their own,
While the wordless worlds that bound him
    Whisper their undertone :
From the hawk and the hound yet clearer
    He hears the secret fall,
Which nearer to him and nearer
    Brings the great God of all.

In the leaves that blow and perish
   In the space of a single hour,
As the loves that most we cherish
   Die like the frailest flower—
In the living things whose living
   Withers or e'er they bloom,
He reads of the great thanksgiving,
   Which breathes from the open tomb.

The bright Spring leaves returning
   To the stem whence Autumn's fell—
And the heart of Summer burning,
   To change at the Winter's spell—:
The year that again repasses—
   The grain that again revives—
Are signs on the darkened glasses
   That bar and bound our lives.

I know how the glass must darken
   To my vision more and more,
When the weak ear strains to hearken,
   And the faint eye glazes o'er:
But the glass shall melt and shiver,
   Once kissed by the fighting breath,
And the light beyond the River
   Shine full in the face of Death.

Strong-set in a strong affection,
   We look to the golden prime,
When a mightier Resurrection
   Shall burst on the doubts of Time;
And the thoughts of all the sages,
   Like the waves of the fretful main,
At the base of the Rock of Ages
   Shall foam and fume in vain.

STANZAS.

Christ is my star—the Light of God,
   To man in mercy given,
To shine beside his wandering road,
   Upon the path to Heaven.

Christ is the Way—the Truth—the Life,
   God's own and only Son,
Our shelter in a world of strife,
   Till that gray world be done.

Christ is the Vine—whose ruddy stream
   To warm our hearts is poured;
Whose quiet branches spread, and seem
   The shadow of the Lord.

Christ is the Master—ever near,
   With lessons soft and mild,
To him who will but kneel, and hear
   Those lessons, like a child!

He asks the child's confiding heart,
    The child's entreating tone,
And will to all Himself impart
    Who lean on Him alone.

What though our wasted years seem dark
    With memories all of ill?
Christ's promise stands as stood the ark,
    And braves the tempest still.

It rides in triumph out and o'er
    Life's wildest, stormiest sea;
And as He hushed the waves of yore,
    Hushed shall our sorrow be.

Turn straight to Him! for His the strength
    That arms our shrinking prayer;
He leads to God Himself at length:
    Pray—for our God is there!

A CHRISTMAS MESSAGE.

THERE was of old a child, born of a maiden,
    Who speaks still from her breast :
"Come to Me all—weary and heavy laden,
    And I will give you rest.

"I give it in My time ; but not, remember,
    At your impatient will,
Changing at once the dull flats of December
    To a spring-girdled hill.

"I could, for power is Mine : but I am Master
    In ways beyond your ken ;
And you must meet storm, sorrow, and disaster,
    Bravely, as honest men.

"Truth, above all, is My own cherished virtue,
    Pure and without alloy ;
And, children, when the world's cold falsehoods hurt you,
    Then let Me be your joy.

"When worthy anger makes you feel as strangers,
    Lost on your devious road,
I, who from God's house scourged the money-changers,
    Whisper: 'Have faith in God.'

"When the dull troubles of the way perplex you,
    Despise them—for you can;
I know the darkest fancies that can vex you,
    Children, for I was man.

"I know the paths of sin, and shame, and sorrow,
    Your careless steps have trod;
But I can change sin's night to sinless morrow,
    Children, for I was God.

"What though two thousand years the world be older,
    With newer sins of men?
I, who to loving hearts grow never colder,
    Am man, as I was then.

"Bring all your thoughts to Me! Doubt not nor tremble;
    On Me your burdens cast;
I, Light of Light, deceive not nor dissemble,
    But am God to the last.

"To your world's last, when I come down to banish
    Your petty doubts and fears,
To bless and crown, while crowns and kingdoms vanish,
    The faith that smiles through tears.

A CHRISTMAS MESSAGE.

"When life seems dark, kneel but in trust before Me,
    You shall not long repine;
When life seems fair, kneel only to adore Me,
    And then its smile is Mine.

"I give not as the world gives—worldly leaven
    Rests on earth's dearest love;
But I have stored My treasure high in Heaven,
    For hearts that dwell above.

"Ask but for Me, and I will not deny you,
    But think and ponder well;
Once let Me hold your heart, and I defy you
    Ever to break the spell!

"I am a jealous God, like the great Father,
    Who never spoke in vain;
And rule o'er those, whom in My fold I gather,
    With undivided reign.

"You cannot loose the plough; you cannot turn you
    From the dear Lord so nigh;
Once let the Master's love inflame and burn you,
    And it shall never die.

"It shall burn on, in ever-kindling splendour,
    Up to the great white throne,
Consuming sin in the flame of self-surrender,
    Through which I claim Mine own.

"Oh fear not, when a strange unbidden ardour
    Spurs you to high desires;
Nor wonder, if the heart seem something harder,
    Even for the cleansing fires.

"Great trials are My angels—sent to prove you,
    And man the soul within,
With thoughts that soar beyond all words, to move you
    To hate the touch of sin.

"When by its weight your earthly reeds are broken,
    Then raise your eyes above:
When man's love fails, remember Who has spoken
    And said—that God is Love.

"Fear not man's judgment; God alone ordaineth
    For your eternal weal;
Your conscience is the court wherein He reigneth,
    From Whom is no appeal.

"And He, who dwells in mystic glory yonder,
    Made Me of human birth,
That as I wandered once, I still may wander
    In search of love on earth.

"Who runs may read; the words my book discloses,
    As truth itself are true:
My yoke is light, My chains are all of roses,
    Whose thorns I wore for you.

"Yield but your heart up as a free oblation
   To Father and to Son;
And you shall learn, in a flash of revelation,
   That we indeed are One.

"When the full heart is sore, and the eye tearful,
   Then are we both most near;
And though your love for very love be fearful,
   Ours shall cast out your fear.

"Forget your follies, doubting son—forgiven,
   When you bowed heart and knee;
Pray but to meet your loved and lost in Heaven,
   And leave the rest to Me."

THE END.

www.ingramcontent.com/pod-product-compliance
Lightning Source LLC
Chambersburg PA
CBHW032138230426
43672CB00011B/2381